CAPTAIN OF ENGLAND
WAYNE
ROONEY

Also by Tom and Matt Oldfield:

Gareth Bale: The Boy Who Became a Galáctico

Raheem Sterling: Young Lion

Cover illustration by Dan Leydon.
To learn more about Dan visit danleydon.com
To purchase his artwork visit etsy.com/shop/footynews
Or just follow him on Twitter @danleydon

CAPTAIN OF ENGLAND
WAYNE
ROONEY

TOM AND MATT OLDFIELD

DINO

Published by Dino Books,
an imprint of John Blake Publishing Ltd,
3 Bramber Court, 2 Bramber Road,
London W14 9PB, England

www.johnblakebooks.co.uk

www.facebook.com/johnblakebooks 🔲
twitter.com/jblakebooks 🔲

This edition published in 2015

ISBN: 978 1 78418 647 0

British Library Cataloguing-in-Publication Data:

A catalogue record for this book is available from the British Library.

Design by www.envydesign.co.uk
Cover illustration by Dan Leydon
Background image Shutterstock

Printed in Great Britain by CPI Group (UK) Ltd

3 5 7 9 10 8 6 4

Papers used by John Blake Publishing are natural, recyclable products made from
wood grown in sustainable forests. The manufacturing processes conform to the
environmental regulations of the country of origin.

Every attempt has been made to contact the relevant copyright-holders, but some
were unobtainable. We would be grateful if the appropriate people could contact us.

To Mum and Dad

For all those mornings and afternoons on the touchline, and for making all of this possible.

TABLE OF CONTENTS

ACKNOWLEDGEMENTS

This was a very special opportunity for us, as brothers, to work together on something we are both so passionate about. Football has always been a big part of our lives. We hope this book will inspire others to start/continue playing football and chasing their dreams.

Writing a book like this was one of our dreams, and we are extremely thankful to John Blake Publishing and Anna Marx, in particular, for making this project possible. Anna's guidance and patience were huge factors in our writing process.

We are also grateful to all the friends and family that encouraged us along the way. Your interest and sense of humour helped to keep us on track. Will, Doug, Mills, John, James Pang-Oldfield and the rest of our King Edward VI friends, our aunts, uncles, cousins, the Nottingham and Montreal families and so many others – thank you all.

Melissa, we could not have done this without your understanding and support. Thank you for being as excited about this collaboration as we were.

Noah, we're already doing our best to make football your favourite sport! We look forward to reading this book with you in the years ahead.

Mum and Dad, the biggest thank you is reserved for you. You introduced us to football and then devoted hours and hours to taking us to games. You bought the tickets, the kits, the boots. We love football because you encouraged us to. Thank you for all the love, all the laughs and for always believing in us. This book is for you.

CHAPTER 1

OLD TRAFFORD'S NEW HERO

'Roo-ney! Roo-ney! Roo-ney!'

It was the sound of 75,000 fans chanting his name. Wayne just stared straight ahead down the tunnel. His heart was beating fast – in fact, it had been pounding since he put on the famous red Manchester United shirt in the dressing room ten minutes earlier. It was a long time since he had felt this nervous about playing football. But then this wasn't just any game.

It was 28 September 2004 and he was just minutes away from the start of his United career. Where was the referee? 'Come on, let's go,' he muttered to himself.

That night's game against Turkish giants Fenerbahce in the Champions League was the start of a new chapter for Wayne. He was following in the footsteps of George Best, Bobby Charlton, Eric Cantona, Bryan Robson and so many other United legends. Now Wayne would have the chance to add his name to that list.

As he thought about his whirlwind journey from the streets of Croxteth in Liverpool to the Theatre of Dreams, he smiled to himself. He had started his first Premier League game for Everton just two years ago and now he was about to make his debut for one of the biggest clubs in the world. The hairs on his neck stood on end.

A broken bone in his foot had delayed his debut and United had begun the new season without him. But all anyone wanted to know was when Wayne would be back. When would United fans get their first glimpse of the teenage sensation who had cost £30 million that summer? And how would he top his incredible performances at Euro 2004?

Wayne wanted to make up for lost time. His foot

had been fine in training this week and he just hoped that there would be no pain once he put it to the test in a real game.

As crowds of United fans walked down Sir Matt Busby Way that night, there was a different buzz in the air. Wayne would be making his debut and they were going to share in that experience. Many of them already had 'Rooney' on the back of their United shirts.

Just before the teams took to the pitch, Ryan Giggs walked up to Wayne and patted him on the back. Maybe he could sense the newcomer's nerves. 'Don't put too much pressure on yourself tonight. Just enjoy it – you only get to make your Manchester United debut once!'

He winked then shook Wayne's hand. 'The club's going to be in your hands some day soon. This is where it all begins for you.'

Finally, the waiting was over. Wayne took a deep breath and stretched his neck to one side and then the other. Showtime.

As he walked across the Old Trafford turf, the

Champions League anthem blared out and caught
Wayne by surprise. It was the first time he had
heard it for one of his games. It always gave him
goosebumps when he heard it on television but it
was a hundred times better in person. That's why I
had to make this move, he reminded himself.

He jumped up and down and did some final
stretches, and as he did so, he spotted his family in
the crowd among the sea of red shirts. His fiancée,
Colleen, was there with them. They were waving
and cheering. The last two months had been difficult
for the whole family and he was happy that they
were with him tonight as he put on the United shirt
for the first time.

Wayne's decision to leave his former club Everton
had shaken the blue half of the city. He had been
called Judas, a traitor and a greedy kid. Wayne would
always love Everton. They had believed in him and
given him a chance to shine. But he just had to take
this next step.

The Old Trafford crowd was so noisy, he didn't
realise that his manager, Sir Alex Ferguson, was on

the touchline and wanted a final word with him. Now aware of him, Wayne ran over. 'You were born to play on this stage, Wayne,' Ferguson said. 'Give these defenders the worst night of their lives. The fans want to see something special, so give them a show to remember.'

The football pitch was always where Wayne felt most at home. As he reached the centre circle for the kick-off with new strike partner Ruud van Nistelrooy, his nerves were replaced with excitement. After all, football had been part of his life from the very start.

CHAPTER 2

A SIGN OF
THINGS TO COME

The Rooneys didn't believe in small parties. A real celebration meant inviting all the cousins, uncles, aunts, grandparents, friends, friends of friends and so on. And Wayne's first birthday in October 1986 was no different.

The planning had started months in advance – finding a date that everyone could make, sending out the invitations, choosing the decorations and the games, and picking the music.

The last item on the list was the birthday cake and Jeanette, Wayne's mother, rushed to pick it up at the local bakery on the morning of the party.

'Don't worry – it's all ready,' the bakery manager

said, seeing the door swing open and sensing her panic. He ducked below the counter and reappeared with a square white box. In dramatic style, he pulled back the lid to reveal a large blue cake. He looked at Jeanette for a sign of approval.

Jeanette smiled. 'It looks delicious,' she said. 'Perfect for an Everton fan.'

'Great – I'll just put "Happy Birthday, Wayne!" on the top and then it's all yours.'

Jeanette paused. 'Oh, actually, could you make it "Happy Birthday, *Little* Wayne!"'

The manager laughed. He was well aware that the Rooney tradition was to give the father's name to the first-born son. 'Good point. You don't want Big Wayne thinking it's for him!'

Jeanette made it home safely with the cake. The aunts and uncles were already there, blowing up balloons and hanging decorations from the curtain rails. The cousins were keeping Little Wayne entertained upstairs so that it would be a surprise – not that he really understood that today was his birthday anyway.

Jeanette saw lots of people in the house but her husband was nowhere to be found. She started to worry. He had been there when she left. Luckily, her sister had an update:

'Big Wayne just called. He'll be back in a minute. He's just picking up that secret present he can't keep quiet about.'

That's a relief, thought Jeanette. She checked her watch. She needed his help with a whole list of jobs before the rest of the guests arrived. And she was eager to find out what this mystery present was – all she knew was that her husband had spotted it recently with his friends.

Ten minutes later, Big Wayne rushed into the kitchen, out of breath. 'Okay, all sorted. Let's get this party started!'

Jeanette explained which jobs were still on her list and then headed upstairs to get Little Wayne dressed. She was pleased to find her son sitting on the floor playing quietly with a tennis ball. It was rare to see him so still rather than scrambling around. He didn't even complain when she changed him out of his pyjamas and into his outfit for the day. Some would have picked out a shirt and trousers for this special occasion, but not the Rooneys. Football would always be number one in this household and there was only one thing suitable for today – his tiny Everton kit.

Finally, the preparations were over and the party could begin. It seemed like the Rooneys had taken over the street for the day, with cars parked everywhere. Family and friends filled the lounge and kitchen, and everyone wanted a glimpse of the birthday boy.

The party was a huge success. The music, the games, the food – it was all exactly as Jeanette had planned. Little Wayne was on his best behaviour, charming everyone with his cheeky grin, complete with six little teeth.

As Jeanette handed out plates of birthday cake and bowls of jelly and ice cream, her mind was already turning towards the big clean-up after the guests had left.

But the party wasn't over yet. A big pile of presents sat unopened on the kitchen table – that was the advantage of having so many aunts, uncles and cousins. Jeanette was one of nine children; Big Wayne was one of eight. It looked like Little Wayne would need a new toy chest. She was glad that they had moved out of their flat and into this house earlier in the year.

Big Wayne couldn't wait any longer. He picked up a long, thin package with blue-and-white wrapping paper: the mystery gift.

'Time for presents!' he announced, with a big smile. 'He has to open this one first.'

Big Wayne dropped the package gently into his son's lap as everyone pulled their chairs forward to form a tight circle around the birthday boy. Little Wayne stared at the wrapping paper and then grabbed clumsily at the edges. Big Wayne crouched down next to his son and helped him undo the pieces of sellotape.

'This is so you'll never forget that you're a blue for life,' Big Wayne said, lifting the present so his son could see it.

It was an Everton sign, in the shape of a car

licence plate. Little Wayne was curious. He reached forward and ran his little fingers along the bumpy surface, perhaps recognising the club crest from all the Everton banners and decorations around the house. His next instinct was to put the sign in his mouth – but Big Wayne moved quickly to stop him.

'You don't want to eat that, little man. You'll crack your teeth!'

Little Wayne giggled.

Jeanette had been standing in the doorway, keeping one eye on Little Wayne as he opened the package and the other on her husband's proud reaction. Now she joined the crowd in the lounge. It had been an eventful year but with every milestone Jeanette felt so lucky. An illness as a child had left her fearing that she would never have children. But then Little Wayne came along.

She was stirred from her daydream by a friendly hand on her shoulder. 'So, he's an Everton fan, then?' her sister asked with a smile.

'As if there could be any other choice!' Jeanette replied, laughing.

One-by-one, the presents were passed forward. Father and son worked together to open each one – but Little Wayne's eyes rarely left his new Everton sign.

An hour later, the guests had gone and the house was quiet again. Little Wayne yawned loudly and rubbed his eyes. 'Bedtime for you – you've had a tiring day,' Big Wayne said, scooping his son out of his playpen and carrying him up the stairs.

He brought the sign with him. Once the birthday boy was in his cot and drifting off to sleep, Big Wayne propped the sign up on the window sill – out of reach but where his son could always see it.

CHAPTER 3

VACUUM TO THE RESCUE

At the Rooneys' three-bedroom house on Armill Road in Croxteth, Wayne got his own room. It made him feel very grown up. He had his own wardrobe, a little bookcase and a chest full of toys. He soon had two little brothers to play with as well – first Graeme and then John.

Even in his earliest years, things came easily for Wayne. He was good at every sport he tried, he showed natural ability at school and he had lots of friends.

But at night he felt lonely and scared. He didn't really understand why. Night after night, he would end up coming into his parents' bed. He couldn't sleep in his room. Sometimes he claimed there was a ghost; sometimes it was a monster under the bed or a werewolf hiding in the darkness. Even his Everton things – his lampshade, his duvet-cover and, of course, the sign on the window sill – couldn't calm his nerves.

'He tries to fall asleep, he really does,' Jeanette told her sister one morning. 'We've tried all kinds of things but it's as if his brain just won't switch off. Then we hear the little patter of footsteps and our bedroom door swings open.'

'Oh dear, poor little lad. Hopefully it's just a phase he's going through. We went through something similar with our little ones.'

'Let's hope it's that. We're trying not to panic too much. Plus, last night was better – Wayne kept the light on and had the television on quietly as well. That seemed to help him. But he'll need to get used to sleeping in the dark at some point.'

Remarkably, despite this lack of sleep, Wayne never felt tired during the day. Every morning he ran down the stairs full of energy, as if the sleepless nights never

happened. He never used it as an excuse to miss
school, and it never slowed him down during the
lunchtime football games in the playground. He lived
for those games, and he would sit in class counting
down the minutes until the bell rang.

Then one afternoon, Wayne found an answer to
his sleeping problem. Jeanette had decided that the
house needed a good clean, from top to bottom,
and a quiet weekend was the perfect opportunity.
She and Big Wayne cleaned, polished and mopped
all morning. Before long, the kitchen counters were
sparkling and the floor was spotless. Time to clean
upstairs, Jeanette decided.

She climbed the stairs and brought the vacuum
cleaner with her, plugging it in on the landing. For
once, Wayne wasn't out playing in the street with his
mates. Instead, he was lying on his bed, bouncing a
little football off the ceiling and humming to himself.

As Jeanette started hoovering the landing and the
entrance to the bathroom, Wayne's eyes gradually felt
heavier and heavier. The sound of the vacuum was
soothing and he closed his eyes. Two minutes later, he

was fast asleep. Jeanette smiled when she peeked into Wayne's bedroom and heard her son snoring.

Wayne didn't understand at first. He thought he had just fallen asleep because he was so tired. Why would he think it was anything else? When he took another long afternoon nap a week later while his dad was hoovering downstairs, Wayne realised that the vacuum was the secret to his deep sleep.

It quickly became part of his routine. After school, he would play football with his mates until it got dark. When it was time for bed, he would plug in the vacuum and drift off to sleep to the sound of his special lullaby. Hairdryers worked as well. Just any kind of background noise that whooshed or buzzed seemed to do the trick. Jeanette and Big Wayne didn't know what to think. They'd never heard of anything like this before. But they weren't complaining.

'Whatever works for you, Wayne,' Jeanette said. 'It's wonderful to see you sleeping more. But one of these days I want you to actually use the vacuum to clean up your room. That's what it's for, after all!'

Before long, the rest of the family had heard all about Wayne's new habit. His cousins thought it was very funny and they teased Wayne about it. Sometimes they would turn on a hairdryer and see if it made him sleepy. 'Don't fall asleep, Wayne,' they would say as they plugged it in.

The noise at night was a small price to pay for Wayne getting more sleep. It didn't seem to disturb Graeme or John, who shared the bedroom next to his. 'Thank goodness we gave Wayne his own room,' Jeanette said to her husband. 'Imagine if one of the other boys was trying to sleep in the room as well! We'll probably sleep better too if Wayne's not climbing into our bed in the middle of the night.'

Big Wayne smiled. 'That's true. I guess that vacuum keeps the ghosts and monsters away! But I'll be worried if we're still having this conversation when he's eighteen!'

CHAPTER 4

A BALL TO
TREASURE

Wayne jumped out of bed when he heard the door-
bell. He never wanted to miss a minute of Uncle
Eugene's visits. When his uncle came to the house,
it usually meant presents – and he always saved the
best ones for Wayne.

'How's my little champ?' his uncle asked as Wayne
flew down the stairs and leapt into his arms.

'Got any sweets?' Wayne asked, flashing a cheeky
grin.

Uncle Eugene laughed. He searched his pockets
and handed Wayne half a packet of Fruit Pastilles.
'Don't tell your mum!' he said, looking around to

check the coast was clear. 'She'll blame me when you have to go to the dentist.'

Wayne's brothers, Graeme and John, raced into the room. The three boys were all in Everton pyjamas and looked more alike than ever. Like Wayne, his siblings didn't want to miss out on presents. They put on big smiles and huddled closer.

'Don't worry, I've got presents for all of you,' Uncle Eugene said, reaching into one of the bags that he had brought with him. 'I always take care of my favourite nephews.'

He handed small parcels to Graeme and John. As they ran to the kitchen to open them, they shrieked with excitement and kept bumping into each other. Then Uncle Eugene turned to Wayne, with a bigger bag in his hand. 'I've got something extra special for you. I know you love football so I thought it was about time that you had one of these. Every six-year-old should have one!'

Wayne grabbed the bag and glanced inside. His eyes were wide open in disbelief.

'A proper ball – a leather one!' he squealed,

running over for a hug. It was the new Mitre ball, just like the one the professionals played with.

'Thanks, Uncle Eugene. I've got to show my mates.' He turned to run away.

'Hang on, Wayne,' Uncle Eugene called. 'The ball comes with one condition – the first time you use it, it has to be at the park with me. I want to see it in action.'

'Sure. It's sunny outside. Can we go now?'

Uncle Eugene laughed at his nephew's enthusiasm. Wayne may have only just woken up and was still in his pyjamas, but he was always ready to play. 'Check with your mum. If she says yes, I'll take you there. I guess I'll have to be in goal, won't I?'

'You're always the goalkeeper. I need to work on my shooting.'

Jeanette said Wayne could go for an hour and he sprinted to the car. An hour was all that he needed. He loved the feeling of smashing the leather ball. He flicked the ball up and volleyed it, he curled it with the inside of his foot and then he jumped up for headers. Uncle Eugene was out of breath as he dived around trying to save Wayne's shots. Usually, he had no chance.

Every time Uncle Eugene picked the ball out of the net and threw it back to Wayne, his nephew had a big grin on his face. The ball was a success.

'Wayne, when you're playing in the Premiership, just remember who got you your first football,' he joked.

That night, Wayne sneaked into the bathroom and washed the mud off his new ball. He wanted it to be shiny for the next day when he would be playing with his mates again. They were going to be really jealous when they saw it. None of them had an expensive one like his.

He dried the ball with a towel and brought it back into his bedroom. As he climbed into bed, he brought the ball with him and tucked it over the duvet next to him, cradling it with his arm. He didn't want to let it out of his sight.

But that ball didn't last long. Nor did the next one. Or the next one. Either Wayne was losing them in neighbours' gardens (one even ended up on the school roof), or he was ripping the leather and wearing them out from playing for hours and hours in the street.

'Not again, Wayne,' Jeanette would say each time, shaking her head. He always had a story about how it wasn't his fault that he had lost the ball. Sometimes he would try to blame it on Graeme or John. At least he was doing something active, she told herself, even if she often feared that a neighbour would call to complain about a broken window or a ruined flowerbed.

One afternoon, Wayne's grandmother heard crying through her kitchen window. Sure enough, it was Wayne. Pretending to be one of his Everton heroes, he had kicked the ball as hard as he could. To his dismay, it flew up and over the fence into the next garden.

Retrieving the ball seemed straightforward, to begin with. Wayne found enough footholds to climb up to the top of the fence and drop down into the garden. But climbing back over was impossible. Every time he tried to jump up, he slid back down. In the end, he gave up and cried out, 'Nan! Nan! I'm stuck. Help!' Tears rolled down his face as he sat on the ground.

His grandmother hurried outside. 'Wayne? What have I told you about playing out there? You can't just climb into other people's gardens. Stay there, I'll ask them to open the side gate.'

'Sorry, Nan,' Wayne said when she appeared. 'I was worried I would lose the ball. They didn't return the last one I kicked over and Mum told me to take better care of this one.'

'That's why you should take the ball to the park if you want to play outside. For a little lad, you kick the ball so hard. Honestly, I don't know what your parents are feeding you!'

But her anger never lasted long. She loved spending time with Wayne, and he knew how to charm his grandmother. An apology and a big smile usually did the trick and within minutes Wayne would be tucking into a bag of sweets.

CHAPTER 5

THE GEMS

The next summer, Wayne found a better option for playing football outside, and it was one where he couldn't get in trouble. The Gems Youth Club behind the Rooneys' house had a tarmac pitch.

Wayne discovered it when he was looking for a ball he had kicked over the back fence. As he tried to guess where it might have landed, he heard voices and the sound of a ball being kicked against a wall.

He pushed his way through some thick bushes and peered over a small fence. He caught a glimpse of a small football pitch with goalposts marked at each end. Three boys were standing in one corner playing with a ball. He knew them from the year above him at school.

Wayne walked round the path until he saw a little opening – just big enough for him to squeeze through. Suddenly, he was on the pitch.

One of the boys looked up.

'Can I play?' Wayne asked.

'Sure. We need another player. We're waiting for a couple of my mates to get here. We should have enough for four-a-side. I'm Joe. What's your name?'

'Wayne. I live just behind here. I've seen you playing at school. I go to St Swithin's as well but I'm in the year below. I'm only seven.'

'Are you any good?'

'I'm one of the best in my year. I've got a really hard shot.'

One of the boys laughed. 'We'll see about that.'

Soon, Joe's friends arrived and they were ready to play. They picked teams. Wayne was the last one to be picked. He couldn't believe it. He was usually picked first. He felt the anger growing inside him. The others would regret it.

Wayne played as well as he had ever played. Some of the boys were jogging, but Wayne was sprinting. Even though he was easily the smallest on the pitch, he wasn't afraid to knock the older boys off the ball.

Within five minutes, Wayne had scored two goals. But he wasn't finished. Joe chipped the ball forward and Wayne chased after it. He controlled it on his thigh and volleyed an unstoppable shot past the keeper into the top corner. He raised his arms. 'Hat-trick!'

Joe ran over. 'Nice one, Wayne. I guess I should have picked you first!'

Wayne smiled. He loved this pitch. He could work on his shooting, he could practise his passing and, best of all, it would be hard to lose the ball.

The game lasted almost an hour. Then the others went home. 'If you ever need another player, knock on my door. It's number twenty-eight,' he said to Joe as the other boys left.

But Wayne still wasn't ready to go home. When he found his lost ball under a neighbour's car, he returned to The Gems, this time alone. He had the whole pitch to himself. He kicked the ball against the wall and moved from side to side to control it as it bounced back. Then he moved further back and picked out a special mark on the wall. He took a run up and aimed his shot to hit the mark.

When he was tired of shooting, he practised his ball control. He flicked the ball up and used his feet, thighs, chest and head to keep the ball in the air, stopping it from hitting the ground. Wayne had seen the Everton players doing this during the warm-up when he went to games at Goodison Park.

In the end, he stayed until it got so dark that he couldn't see the ball clearly anymore.

After that, he was always at The Gems. When it was time for dinner, Jeanette would go to the bottom of the stairs and call Wayne to the table. If he wasn't in his room, she knew where to find him. She would go to the back door and shout his name. Five minutes later, Wayne would be back from The Gems, washing his hands and sitting down at the table.

'At least we always know where he is,' she said

to her husband one night. 'And it's safer than him playing in the street.'

Before long, Wayne was the one arranging the games at The Gems. He would go from door to door, asking if his mates were home and wanted to play. In the summer holidays, when school shut down for two months, there were eleven-a-side games every day. There was hardly room to move on the little pitch but that helped Wayne to create space for himself. He had to be quick on his feet to avoid being kicked in the ankles. Sometimes, girls from his school would come to watch the games, and Wayne always made sure that he put on a good show in front of them.

Wayne was rarely on the losing team – and that was just as well because he didn't take losing well. Whether it was throwing his boots or kicking the goalposts, Wayne's temper could be scary. His friends quickly understood how badly he wanted to win, even just in games at The Gems.

One afternoon, Big Wayne finished work early. When he got home, the house was empty. He decided to walk over to The Gems. Maybe Wayne knew where everyone was.

Big Wayne had seen his son playing football in the street before and he had taken Wayne to the park many times, but this was the first time he had watched him play at The Gems.

When he got there, he sat on a wooden bench. Wayne didn't see him, as he was focused on the game. The ball bounced off the wall and into Wayne's path. He turned and dribbled past one defender. As another of them ran over, he faked to go left, then darted right. With just the goalkeeper to beat, he didn't panic. He calmly curled the ball past the keeper. Big Wayne grinned. His son was the best player on the pitch.

When dinner time brought an end to the game, Wayne finally spotted his dad on the bench. How long had he been there, he wondered?

'Wayne, that was incredible,' his dad said. 'They couldn't get the ball off you.'

'They tried but I was too quick,' Wayne said, with a confident smile. 'But it wasn't a real game. We were just messing around.'

'Well, I think it's time you tested yourself in a real game for a real team with a real coach.'

Wayne hesitated. He wasn't sure if he was ready for that, but he loved playing football. 'Do you know a team that's looking for players?'

'A friend told me about a youth team run by our local pub. The team is called Copplehouse. I'm going to call the manager tonight.'

CHAPTER 6

CATCHING
THE EYE

Big Nev, the Copplehouse Under-9s manager, blew his whistle and waved the boys towards him. The warm-up was over. Wayne scooped up his water bottle and jogged over with his teammates. He had been unsure about joining the team when his father suggested it, but now he loved it.

'Today's a big one, boys,' Big Nev explained. 'This team is above us in the table but we're just as good as them. Play your best and we'll beat them.'

As the referee blew his whistle and the boys walked away to take up their positions on the pitch, he added: 'Hang on, one more thing. I heard that scouts from Liverpool and Everton might be showing up today – so there's some extra motivation for you.'

Wayne's eyes lit up. People from Everton? At one of his games?

It didn't take long for him to make his mark. He won a tackle on the halfway line, raced past two defenders and fired a low shot from the edge of the penalty area. It flew into the bottom corner. There was no big celebration, just a smile and a clenched fist as his teammates ran over to congratulate him.

In the second half, he scored again. This time, he played a clever one-two on the edge of the box and slipped the ball through the goalkeeper's legs. The defenders looked like statues as Wayne ran rings round them. Sometimes it seemed as if the ball was attached to his foot.

As the game entered the final few minutes, Copplehouse clung to a 2-1 lead. Most of the parents were nervously counting down the seconds. But Big Wayne's attention was distracted by the sight of a white-haired man walking behind one of the goals, who seemed to be staring back at him.

Big Wayne moved nearer to the mysterious white-haired man, who slowed down and stopped. As the referee blew the final whistle, Big Wayne paused for a second to clap the Copplehouse players. Most of them were running over to Wayne, wanting to share the moment with the 'man of the match'.

'Are you Wayne's dad?' the old man asked.

'Yeah, that's me,' Big Wayne replied cautiously, turning around.

'He's quite a player – lovely touch, never stops running. I had to come over and talk to you. You see, I'm a scout for Liverpool and we'd love to bring him in for a trial.'

Forgetting for a moment that he had spent most of his life thinking of the Liverpool team as the enemy, Big Wayne felt excitement and pride.

'Nice to meet you,' he said, shaking the scout's hand. 'Wayne definitely picked the right game to score those goals. He's going to be over the moon.'

'Great. Here's my card.' The Liverpool scout handed over a business card and took a notepad from his back pocket. 'If you scribble your phone number down, I'll be in touch tomorrow.'

A minute later, the Liverpool scout was just leaving when Wayne raced over. Looking down at the red-faced nine-year-old, he said, 'We'll see you up at Melwood, Wayne. Great game today.' Then he marched off towards his car.

Confused, Wayne looked at his dad for answers. 'Who was that?'

'Who?' his father asked, pretending not to know what his son was talking about.

Wayne waved his arms impatiently. 'You know who. That man you were just talking to.'

'Are you ready to hear this? He's a scout at Liverpool. You caught his eye with those cracking goals and they want you to go and train there next week.'

'Liverpool?' Wayne asked, unsure of how to react. Usually his dad didn't like talking about Liverpool.

'This is a great opportunity, son. Try not to think about the rivalry with Everton.'

But when Wayne arrived at Liverpool's training

ground, something felt wrong. Maybe it was just nerves. Maybe it was some of the things he'd heard his family say about Liverpool. Or maybe it was the funny looks he was getting for showing up in his Everton kit.

Two of the Liverpool coaches stood together by one of the corner flags and watched him. 'He better be some player showing up in that kit,' one said to the other.

Even though he felt a bit uncomfortable, Wayne played well, and started to impress the coaches.

'I've been watching him – he's special,' one of the coaches confided to his colleague. 'His technique is excellent and he's too good for the other kids in the five-a-side games. Even if he's an Everton fan, we should bring him back next week for another look before making a decision.'

When Wayne got home, two of his older cousins were in the living room. They wanted to know all about the trial.

'I don't know how I feel,' Wayne said, collecting his thoughts. 'It was strange having a trial for

Liverpool. As an Everton fan, I felt guilty – like I was letting my team down. But Liverpool want me back for another session next week and then I'll find out if I got a place at their Centre of Excellence.'

CHAPTER 7

BECOMING A BLUE

One telephone call changed everything. Wayne could only hear his dad's side of the conversation, but he sounded excited.

'Yes, he'd love that'… 'Well, he's got another trial there next week before they make an offer'… 'But this is the one he really wants'… 'Oh yes, that would be great'.

Finally, Wayne lost patience. He couldn't take the suspense anymore. Tapping at his dad's arm again and again, he mouthed, 'What? What?'

He eventually got his answer: Everton had also seen his game for Copplehouse, and they wanted him to come for a trial as well.

Wayne asked his dad to repeat the news three times before he believed it was true. He had been noticed by the team he loved – the team that he prayed would win every Saturday, the team that his dad had taken him to watch as a baby. He couldn't wait to tell his mates.

Later that week, Wayne and his father headed for Bellefield, Everton's training ground. Wayne was quiet on the way there. It all still felt like a dream. 'Good luck, son. Show Everton you're the star they've been waiting for.' Big Wayne ruffled his son's hair as he got out of the car.

Wayne felt right at home at Bellefield. The photos on the wall showed some of Everton's greatest moments, many of which he had seen in his dad's scrapbooks. Breathing the same air and walking on the same turf as his idols gave Wayne goosebumps.

On a quick introductory tour, he saw the cafeteria, the changing rooms and from one window, he could see the pitches, with freshly painted white lines. One coach was busy laying out cones while another pumped up the last couple of footballs and added them to a big pile. And all the special, distinctive smells were there – Deep Heat muscle spray, new leather footballs and freshly cut grass. Wayne never wanted to leave. Rain was falling steadily outside but he barely noticed.

It took about fifteen minutes for Everton to realise that they had hit the jackpot. And they weren't about to let Wayne slip through their fingers.

In theory, the other boys at the trial were his rivals but it was hard to think that way when so many of them were Everton fans like him. During the technique drills, he had an extra spring in his step – heading, passing, volley lay-offs. He almost broke the goalkeeper's hand with a volley in the shooting session.

When the five-a-side games started, Andy Windsor was the only coach overseeing Wayne's pitch. Before long, five coaches were huddled on the touchline, nudging each other excitedly.

'You'd think he was a few years older than the rest of the boys,' Andy said. 'They can't get near him.'

'I heard Liverpool are looking at him too, though,'

another coach replied. 'That would be a disaster. Imagine if we lost him to the enemy! We can't let him leave tonight without discussing Centre of Excellence forms.'

Ray Hall, Everton's Youth Development Officer, suddenly appeared behind the group of coaches. He had been watching from the other end of the pitch. 'We won't. I'm going to handle this one myself.'

Ray made sure the Rooneys understood that Everton was the best place for Wayne. He knew that they were big Everton fans and would probably need little persuasion, but this was not the time to take anything for granted. There was a potential superstar up for grabs.

'We treat the boys well at the Centre of Excellence,' he explained. 'The sessions are hard work but we try to keep it interesting. Wayne showed tonight that he would shine here. Think it over and let me know if you have any questions. We'll send a letter in the post and we can take it from there.'

The waiting was the hardest part for Wayne.

He rushed home from school every day to check the post. If the letter hadn't arrived, he feared that Everton had changed their mind about him or that another boy had caught their attention.

At last, an envelope arrived with the Everton crest on it.

'It's here!' Wayne shouted, opening the letter. He sprinted into the kitchen to show his parents. 'I got a place at Everton's Centre of Excellence for next season!'

Wayne had told all his friends and family the good news as soon as Ray Hall confirmed Everton's interest straight after the trial – but, without a letter of confirmation, some of them didn't believe him. Seeing the words in print made it feel real.

'This is huge, Wayne,' Uncle Eugene said excitedly when he heard the news. 'If you keep at it, you can make it. I mean it. Some kids have to make it to the Premier League level – why not you?'

'He's right,' Big Wayne added. 'One day some kids could have posters of you on their bedroom walls.'

Wayne giggled at that idea. But it made him think

about what that poster might look like. Maybe a goal celebration? Or a volley? Or a diving header? As long as he was wearing an Everton shirt, he didn't care.

His first season at Everton's Centre of Excellence confirmed that he belonged. Wayne worked hard in training – three nights a week – but he was always counting the minutes until Sunday morning because that meant real matches against other Under-10 Centre of Excellence teams. And he always saved his best for those matches.

Wayne made that Everton team unstoppable. He just couldn't stop scoring, starting with a hat-trick in his very first game. Big Wayne was keeping a running tally.

'Counting the nine goals against Preston, that's twenty-four goals in five games so far. Have you ever thought about going easy on some of these poor defenders?'

Wayne grinned and shook his head. 'Never.'

One of the games that Wayne had circled on the calendar was against Manchester United. Even though it was only the Under-10s, United were known for their excellent youth academy and were the team to beat in English football. Wayne expected a tough game.

As he warmed up, Wayne felt the excitement building. He didn't even feel cold, despite the chilly wind. 'I want to make them jealous that I'm not part of their Centre of Excellence,' he had told his dad in the car on the way to the game. He looked across the pitch and saw the United players passing the ball back and forth in a circle. Most of them seemed small and some of them were wearing gloves. Wimps, he thought. No matter how cold it got, Wayne would never wear gloves.

Everton's games usually followed a similar pattern. Wayne would score a couple of early goals, the opposition would lose hope and Everton would get an easy win. That's exactly what happened against United. Wayne's first goal was a tap-in. He preferred the spectacular ones but they all counted. Two minutes later, he fired a shot from the edge of the box that flew past the goalkeeper and into the net. He wasn't even sweating yet.

The United defenders tried their best to stop Wayne but he was too strong and too quick. When Everton built a big lead, Wayne liked to try some of the things he had worked on in training – mainly just to show off. A high cross gave him that chance against United. A defender tried to head the ball away but it looped up just behind Wayne as he ran into the box. In an instant, he stopped, swivelled and whipped an overhead kick over the hand of the diving keeper and into the top corner.

Wayne ended up on the ground on his back but before he could turn to see the ball in the net, he heard a roar from the touchline. Coaches and parents from both teams were clapping. John and Graeme, who had made the trip with Big Wayne, were jumping up and down and yelling. Wayne's teammates dived on top of him and he was buried at the bottom of the pile. He smiled as he jogged back to the centre circle. He would never forget that goal.

After that, Wayne just kept scoring. In some games it was six goals, in others it might be eight or nine. By the end of the season, he had scored 114 goals in twenty-nine games. He was making it all look so easy.

'Son, that was an amazing season,' said Big Wayne. 'I hope you realise how special it was. Now, let's see if you can beat that next year!'

'If they offer me a place for next year, you mean,' Wayne said. 'The letters are supposed to arrive this week but mine hasn't come yet.'

'Trust me, you don't have to worry about that. You're a goal machine. They want you to be at Everton for a long time.'

But there was always a little doubt in the back of Wayne's mind – even as a nine-year-old, even after all the goals he had scored. Any time he saw a coach talking to his dad, he wondered if it was good or bad news. After most training sessions, he wondered if he had been one of the better players or if others were making faster progress.

His dad was proved right two days later when the letter of confirmation landed on the hallway carpet. Wayne opened it with shaking hands and then called his dad to share the news.

'Everton's letter just arrived. They want me back for next season. But it's even better than that. They want me in the Under-12s, not the Under-11s!'

CHAPTER 8

MASCOT MISCHIEF

Being part of the Centre of Excellence put Wayne
in a good position to chase his dreams of playing
for Everton. But it also brought other benefits. One
of them was the chance to be a ball boy or even a
mascot for an Everton game. Wayne had been a ball
boy a couple of times and he loved being so close to
his heroes.

Finally, a letter arrived with the news he'd been
praying for. He was going to be a mascot – and not
just for any game, but for the Merseyside derby
against Liverpool at Anfield!

'Do you realise how lucky you are, Wayne?' Uncle
Eugene said, grinning. 'A lot of kids would bite their

arm off to be a mascot for the Merseyside derby. You better bring us good luck!'

Wayne couldn't wait for the big day to arrive. He started a countdown on a sheet of paper and crossed off the days one by one. He rehearsed what he would say to each player, especially Dave Watson, the team's captain, who would be walking onto the pitch next to him. Maybe the players had heard about all the goals Wayne was scoring for the Centre of Excellence teams.

But bad weather was about to ruin Wayne's plans. The night before the game, the rain had been keeping him awake, and when morning came, pouring rain was still lashing against his bedroom window. He looked out into the garden and saw puddles forming everywhere. At first, he wasn't worried. He had seen games played in the rain lots of times. Even his games didn't get cancelled because of bad weather.

The weather forecast remained grim, though. When Wayne and his parents left the house and drove to Anfield, the rain continued to be heavy.

The traffic was slower than usual, and there was even thunder and lightning on the way. When they reached the car park at the ground, Wayne spotted the sign for reception and raced out of the car. But he returned ten minutes later looking miserable.

Big Wayne rolled down the window, letting raindrops splash into the car. 'What's wrong?'

'The game is off,' Wayne said in a quiet, sad voice. 'I've been looking forward to this for weeks. It's not fair.'

He climbed into the back seat, slammed the door and burst into tears. He sat in silence all the way home and then ran up to his room.

Jeanette gave him space for a few minutes and then went to see him. Wayne buried his head in his mum's jumper and cried again. Jeanette wrapped her arms around him and stroked his back. 'Wayne, it's going to be OK. You'll see. These things happen. I know you're upset now but you will get another chance. You'll be a mascot for another game.'

Wayne felt better after that. His mum always knew the right things to say.

Fortunately, Wayne received another letter telling him when the postponed match would be played. He had to restart the countdown.

Time seemed to move so slowly. It felt like forever before the date of the game finally arrived. Wayne barely slept the night before. Not even the vacuum could help. He laid out his Everton kit on his chair and wondered what it would be like to walk out onto the pitch with the Everton players. He got dressed hours in advance and then paced his bedroom waiting for his parents to get home from the supermarket. He talked to himself in the mirror and worked on his handshake.

Wayne arrived at Anfield in a bubbly mood. Nothing could spoil this moment. Chris, the Liverpool representative, met him at the reception desk and gave him a quick tour on the way to a small room with refreshments: orange juice and biscuits. He would wait here until it was time to join the players in the tunnel.

Time stood still. 'How much longer?' he kept asking others in the room. He was soon joined by the Liverpool mascot – a skinny boy with blond hair. But Wayne stayed on the other side of the room. It was the Merseyside derby. He didn't want to make friends with a Liverpool fan.

Shortly after, a woman appeared with a trolley. It was the pre-match meal. Wayne had a plate of fish-and-chips and a can of Coke. 'I could get used to this!' he told Chris when he returned.

Finally, the mascots were called. Wayne was guided through two winding corridors and then through a side door into the tunnel. And, just like that, the players were lined up right in front of him. He felt his legs shaking. All the things he had planned to say just slipped from his mind.

He was introduced to Everton captain Dave Watson and they shook hands. Dave asked Wayne whether he was enjoying the youth team training and games. Wayne nodded but when he opened his mouth to speak, no words came out. 'Yeah, I love it,' he finally managed to say.

Wayne couldn't help but stare at the other players in the tunnel, who seemed bigger and stronger than on television. He felt tiny. Liverpool captain John Barnes was right next to him, within touching distance. Wayne tried to pay attention to every little detail so he could tell his family and his mates about it all. They would want to hear the whole story.

Suddenly, the referee gave a quick hand gesture and the players started moving down the tunnel. Dave Watson put a hand on Wayne's back and guided him out onto the pitch. Once there, everywhere he looked, Liverpool fans were cheering their team and booing the Everton players. It was the loudest noise Wayne had ever heard.

As the other players went through their final preparations, Wayne's job was to kick a few balls to Everton goalkeeper Neville Southall as part of his warm-up. It was part of the mascot experience. He had watched other mascots do it before – he knew how it worked. The idea was that Southall would roll the ball out slowly and Wayne would hit a shot back. But Wayne didn't want to just be like all of the others. He had something special and memorable up his sleeve.

When Southall threw the ball to him, he was expecting a few gentle shots. After knocking a few shots back, Wayne sensed it was time for his moment. He dipped his foot under the ball and chipped it over Southall's head and into the net. Some of the fans behind the goal saw it and gave him a big cheer. He beamed.

'Cheeky little brat,' Southall mumbled as he picked the ball out of the net.

Wayne was saved by the referee's whistle. He was called to the centre circle for the coin toss and a photo with the captains. This one is going on my wall, he thought to himself.

Everyone had seen Wayne's rebellious moment, and he worried that he might be in trouble, and that Southall might make a complaint about him. But back in the tunnel, everyone was just smiling. He was in the clear.

'You couldn't help yourself, could you?' Chris said. 'I have to admit, I've never seen anyone do that before.'

'I wanted to make it extra special. Now I can tell my mates I scored a goal at Anfield!'

'Southall didn't look happy. For a second, I thought he was going to chase after you.'

Wayne grinned. 'No chance. He wouldn't have caught me!'

He had a taste for it now. He promised himself that one day he would put on an Everton shirt for a Merseyside derby.

'Let's get going,' Chris said. 'I'll show you where you're sitting for the game. We've got matchday programmes for you too.'

'Great.'

'And try not to cause any trouble on the way,' he said, smiling at the boy.

CHAPTER 9

A FAMILY MOMENT TO REMEMBER

'Boys, sit still!' Jeanette shouted. 'I won't tell you again. Graeme, let go of his arm and move nearer to Wayne.'

Today was a proud day for the whole Rooney family and Jeanette wanted a photo to mark the occasion. Wayne was still the star member of the Everton Centre of Excellence but, when his place was confirmed for the next season, no fewer than three envelopes landed on the Rooneys' doormat. Graeme and John had both been to trials at Everton. Now, like Wayne, they would also be part of its Centre of Excellence.

'I just want one photo, is that too much to ask?'

Jeanette pleaded. 'Show me the letters. John, yours is upside down.'

Wayne and Graeme giggled and tried to help their brother. 'Don't rip my letter!' John screamed. That just made Wayne and Graeme giggle even more.

Hearing all the noise, Big Wayne walked into the room to help his wife. He was still on cloud nine after hearing the news. Weekends would never be the same again, but he loved watching his sons play football. 'Stop messing around and listen to your mum,' he said firmly. 'You'll thank her one day when you've got this photo for your collection.'

The boys sat up straight and held up their letters, just as Jeanette had asked. All three were wearing their Everton kit. They looked like the happiest boys in the world. She smiled. It was a perfect photo. She would get it printed and framed for the wall. Maybe she could put it in the family Christmas card as well, she thought.

'I can't believe we're all going to be playing for Everton next season,' Wayne said excitedly. 'It's amazing! You're going to love it, I promise.'

'It's perfect,' Big Wayne added. 'Three Rooneys – one defender, one midfielder, one striker. Everton will be set for the future.'

'I'm the striker,' Wayne answered quickly.

'No, I am,' Graeme replied. 'I hate defending.'

'Want to bet on who will score the most goals?'

Graeme and John went quiet. They were both promising young players but neither wanted to bet against Wayne. Their brother could score ten goals in one game. People were already saying that Wayne would be the youngest player to ever play for the Everton first team. It wasn't easy to compete with that.

'Just make sure you play well,' Wayne added with a big smile. 'I don't want you to make me look bad.'

Big Wayne walked over and sat down next to his wife. 'Looks like we'll need to plan carefully for the weekends if we need to be in three places at once!'

Jeanette rolled her eyes. 'I guess we can forget about our plans for a weekend away together. Maybe next year.'

There had been initial excitement when the letters arrived, but Graeme and John became nervous when

the first training sessions got nearer and nearer.
Wayne usually loved to tease his brothers at every
opportunity but he knew this was a time to be a
supportive big brother.

'Wayne, what kind of exercises will they get me to
do?' Graeme asked one afternoon. 'Will it be like the
trial where we just played a game the whole time or
is it different?'

'Usually it's a mixture of things. Some running,
some technique drills – passing, heading, shooting –
and then a few five-a-side games. But don't think too
much about it yet. You'll be fine when you get there.
They wouldn't have invited you if they didn't think
you were a good player.'

Graeme beamed. Coming from Wayne, that meant
a lot. He wouldn't say that kind of thing if he didn't
mean it.

'The other thing is to remember to enjoy it,' added
Wayne. 'Everything goes so fast that sometimes I
forgot to enjoy every minute of it at the beginning.
We're really lucky – think of how many of our mates
would love to be training with Everton!'

'Yeah, my mates are really jealous,' replied Graeme. 'They all love Everton. Now I'll get to tell them stories about all the behind-the-scenes action!'

Once the season started, Wayne tried to keep track of how his brothers were doing. At family mealtimes, all the conversations were about the Centre of Excellence – who was doing well, where their games were at the weekend and so on. But Wayne's main focus was his own team and his own progress. He had even given up boxing to focus all his energy on football. Despite playing against older boys, he was the best player on the pitch in almost every game. He wasn't just scoring goals, he was setting up his teammates too.

On one occasion, late in the season, Wayne was leaving training after staying behind for extra shooting practice when he heard a familiar voice calling him. He turned around to see Ray Hall standing in the doorway, signalling for him to come over.

'I just wanted to tell you how impressed we all are with your hard work – not just in the games at the weekend but in training too. Keep it up. There is no limit to how good you can be if you stay focused.'

Wayne grinned. 'Thanks, Mr Hall. I'm going to do whatever it takes to make it to the top, I can promise you that.'

CHAPTER 10

ADAPTING IN DALLAS

'Where's Dallas?' Wayne asked suddenly at the breakfast table one morning.

'America,' Jeanette replied. 'Near the bottom, I think. Why do you ask?'

Wayne unfolded a sheet of paper from his pocket. 'I got this at training last night. There's a tournament in Dallas and Everton is sending a team. I'm part of the squad.'

Jeanette got up and read the rest of the sheet over Wayne's shoulder.

'Wow, that's a long way to go for a tournament. It says you'll be staying with a family in Dallas. That will be different. I bet it will be really hot in the summer.'

'It's going to be boring. I don't want to be away from my mates. What if this family doesn't like football?'

'I'm sure some of the other boys will be staying with families in the same area. Oh, did you read the last part, Wayne?'

Wayne looked. He rolled his eyes. It said he had to write a letter to this mystery family to tell them about himself. He sighed. He hated writing.

'What am I going to say?' he asked, looking at his parents for answers.

'You can tell them that you're thirteen years old and you play for Everton. And you can tell them why you like football so much.'

'And they'll want to know about your family and what kind of food you like,' Big Wayne added.

'You can't tell them you think they're boring, though!' Jeanette joked.

Wayne laughed. His mum was probably right about that.

Writing the letter wasn't as bad as he thought it would be. But it took him three attempts to write it neatly and with the words in a straight line.

When the time came to set off for America, Wayne was laughing and joking in the car on the way to the airport, but he went quiet once it was time to say goodbye to his family. 'I'm going to miss you,' he mumbled. He hugged his mum and dad and waved to his brothers. He could feel the tears coming but he was determined to be brave.

The flight to Dallas was the longest Wayne had ever taken. He was restless and the man in front of him kept tilting his seat. Wayne banged his knee into the back of it from time to time just to get some payback. There was no chance of falling asleep so he tried to watch some films to pass the time.

When the plane landed at the airport, Wayne was welcomed by the family he would be staying with. They had made a special banner so he would know who they were. Their house was beautiful and they gave Wayne a tour. His bedroom was big and he had a bathroom just across the corridor.

'We're really happy to have you staying with us, Wayne. Is there anything else you need?'

'I'd love a nap!' Wayne said with a smile. 'That flight was really tiring.'

Wayne slept for a couple of hours. When he woke up he felt really homesick. He missed his own room, his brothers, his parents and his mates. He missed being able to hop over the fence to The Gems.

When he sat down with the family for dinner, he wasn't hungry. He thought he might be sick if he tried to eat anything. But they served up huge portions and he didn't want to be rude. In the end, he just ate half of his plate of food. How am I going to last two weeks, he wondered?

But once the tournament started, he felt better. The Dallas family was so nice and he got along well with their two children, Jason and Susan. Jason was the same age as Wayne and he wanted to learn more about football – or 'soccer' as he kept calling it. At first, though, they had a hard time understanding Wayne's accent.

'Wayne, come outside,' Jason said after dinner one night. 'Let's play basketball.'

There was a basketball hoop in the driveway and

Jason disappeared into the garage and came back with a basketball that looked worn out from daily use. A bit like one of my footballs, Wayne thought to himself.

'Take a shot, Wayne,' Jason said, throwing him the ball.

Wayne had only played basketball a couple of times at school. He didn't know how to shoot. He just threw the ball towards the hoop but his shot missed completely. Jason laughed.

'Have another go. Shoot it with the fingertips and flick your wrist.'

Wayne took ten more shots. All of them missed and only one of them even hit the rim.

'Let me try something a bit different,' he said, taking ten steps backwards into the street. 'I bet I'll be better with my feet than my hands.'

He placed the basketball on the pavement and gave himself a little run up. Jason watched him in amazement.

Wayne chipped the basketball high into the air. He and Jason watched the ball loop up and then start to fall, as if in slow motion. The basketball swished through the hoop.

'Whoa!!!!!' Jason yelled. 'That was amazing!'

Wayne stood with his arms in the air. 'I told you! These feet are magical!'

Everton would do well at the tournament. Wayne scored two goals in the first game and another in the second game, and the team finished top of their group to qualify for the knockout round. But there was no perfect ending – they lost on penalties in the semi-final. The heat was hard to get used to and Wayne felt more out of breath than he ever did in England.

For Wayne, visiting Dallas had been a fun experience. He had learned a lot, tried new food and enjoyed the feel of American dollars in his hand. But when the plane landed back in England, he was glad to be home.

CHAPTER 11

AN INJURY NIGHTMARE

As Wayne settled back into his old routine and prepared for the new season, he hoped to land more team opportunities with the older age groups, maybe even with the Everton reserves. He loved the challenge of proving himself against bigger, stronger players. He was never afraid.

But in the first training session at the Centre of Excellence, Wayne felt a sharp pain in his right knee. He tried to keep running but every step made him bite his lip to stop himself from yelling. Two minutes later, he limped to the touchline.

'What happened, Wayne?' a concerned coach asked. 'I'm calling the physio.'

'No, don't bother. It's nothing. I must have twisted funny and I got a bit of pain in my knee. It's better now.'

But it wasn't really. He tried to hide it by keeping things simple and playing quick passes so he didn't have to run. After the next session, though, he felt the same pain in his left knee as well. He could hardly move, but he didn't want to admit it.

Joseph, one of the other boys in Wayne's group and one of his best friends on the team, knew something was wrong. Usually, Wayne was firing shots from every angle and racing all over the pitch, but lately it was as if he wasn't trying.

When Wayne went over to get a drink of water, Joseph noticed he was limping. 'Wayne, if you've got an injury, you should tell them about it. No one is going to blame you. Get the physio to take a look. You might be making it worse by pretending there's nothing wrong.'

Wayne shook his head. 'I'm fine. If I go to the physio, he'll tell me to rest it. I won't be able to play. I can't risk it. Plus, maybe it will fix itself.'

But the limping just got worse. Next, his back started hurting as well. It was time to be honest and work out what the problem was, so he told Big Wayne. 'Dad, I'm in agony. My knees are messed up and now my back is really painful as well. It's been like this for two weeks. What if it's serious? What if I can't play anymore?'

'Slow down, son. I didn't realise you had an injury. What did the physio say?'

'I haven't seen him yet.'

'Why not?'

'I was scared. I don't want to lose my place. I've worked so hard and I've got a chance to push for the Under-18s this season. A bad injury could ruin everything.'

'Knowledge is power, son. It might be nothing but you need to get it checked. You're still so young and your body is still developing. Trust me, an injury isn't going to change the way Everton think about you.'

Wayne looked at the ground and nodded.

One phone call later, Wayne had an appointment booked with the academy physio for the following

day. He couldn't sleep that night – but not because
of his knees or his back. He just kept imagining what
could be wrong. Maybe he would need surgery.
What would he do if the physio said his dream of
playing for the Everton first team was over?

When he entered the physio's room, he was just
desperate to get some answers. He lay down on the
soft bench while the physio went through some
gentle exercises to work out exactly where the
pain was coming from. He moved the boy's knees
in different directions and put pressure in specific
places. Some of the exercises didn't hurt at all, but
others made him flinch.

'Right, Wayne,' the physio said after ten minutes
of tests. 'You can sit up. There's good news and less
good news. Which do you want first?'

'The good news.'

'Okay, you'll be pleased to hear that there's no
serious damage. In fact, this is something that a
lot of youngsters go through during growth spurts,
especially boys who play a lot of sport. It's called
Osgood-Schlatter disease and it's the cause of all the

pain you're feeling at the moment. I've had three other Centre of Excellence lads in here with the same thing this week.'

'What was the name?'

'Osgood-Schlatter. It's basically inflamed ligament and it's something we have to be careful with. You need to rest – that's the less good news. I know that will be hard for you but that's the only way to get rid of the pain. I'm afraid there's no magic cure for this. I'm recommending three weeks of rest and then I'll see how you're doing. If things are better, you can start training again.'

Wayne went quiet. It was a relief to know that it wasn't a serious injury but three weeks without football seemed like a disaster. He was used to playing football every morning, afternoon and evening. What was he going to do? Most of all, he hated the idea of missing Centre of Excellence games. He would have to watch from the touchline while someone else took his place.

The days dragged by slowly. After a month of rest, Wayne felt a lot better. He was nervous that the pain might return when he resumed training, but within minutes, he was charging after the ball, and his knees felt fine. By the end of the session, he had totally forgotten about the injury and he felt as sharp as he had before the pain in his knees started. He was back!

He made up for lost time in the weekend matches, scoring four hat-tricks and reclaiming his place as the team's star player. Still, the injury had taught him a valuable lesson: his dreams could be snatched away in an instant. Sport could be cruel like that.

'I've just got to make every minute count,' he told his mum one night as they watched television. 'Injuries are so unfair. I don't ever want to be watching from the touchline again.'

CHAPTER 12

MOYES'S MAGIC WORDS

Now sixteen years old, Wayne knew people were starting to talk about him as a future star of football. He was part of the Everton team which had reached the FA Youth Cup Final against Aston Villa. He had been hoping to play as well as he possibly could, especially as both legs of the final were being televised, but he felt frustrated as deep down, he knew that the opposition had been the better team.

With some help from his cousin, he had even prepared a T-shirt that he wore under his Everton shirt with the message 'Always a blue!' If he scored, he was going to lift up his shirt and show off the T-shirt for the cameras. 'The Everton fans will love it,' he had predicted proudly. But things had not gone to plan.

Sitting on the muddy pitch at an almost empty Villa Park, Wayne replayed some of the key moments in the game over and over in his head. Could he have done more? Would things have been different if he had taken his chances in the first half? With a bit more luck, he could have scored a hat-trick.

As he trudged back into the dressing room, he tried to stay positive. It had been a great run, even if the fairy-tale ending had slipped through his fingers. At least being named Player of the Final was a small consolation prize.

All around him, his teammates were as frustrated as he was. They threw off their shin pads and kicked their dirty kit into the middle of the floor. This Everton team wasn't used to losing – and now they would have to wait until next season to get revenge. It was going to be a long summer.

Suddenly, the conversations stopped and the dressing room went quiet. Wayne was hunched forward, removing the tape from his socks, and at first his view was blocked. He sat up and peered to his right.

Then it all made sense. David Moyes had walked in. He was standing near the door in an Everton tracksuit, with his hands in his pockets, talking to the youth coaches.

Moyes had taken over as Everton manager a couple of months earlier and Wayne had already met him once. Some of his teammates looked at the ground nervously but he felt confident enough to walk over and say hello.

'Hello Wayne – tough luck out there tonight,' Moyes said when the youngster appeared by his side. 'Don't forget how good your season was. We're very proud of what this group has achieved.'

Wayne gave a slight smile. 'Thanks. I've loved it this season. We just didn't want it to end like this.'

Moyes nodded and then gestured for Wayne to join him outside the dressing room to continue the conversation. Once in the hallway, he checked that no one could overhear them, and added: 'I've had some great reports about you. I've already watched videos of a lot of your games and I've kept a close eye on you since I got to Everton. I think it's time to test yourself at the next level.'

'I'm ready!' Wayne interrupted, hoping he sounded confident but not cocky.

'Good, because you'll be training with the first team next season.'

Wayne's jaw dropped. He couldn't think of a single word to say. It wasn't as if he had never thought such a thing was possible. He had overheard his family wondering aloud if it might happen and he knew that some of the radio shows were calling for him to get a chance in the first team. But it was still an incredible feeling to hear it straight from the Everton manager's mouth.

In an instant, he had almost forgotten about the disappointment of losing the FA Youth Cup Final.

'Don't let it go to your head and keep it to yourself for now,' Moyes told him. 'We just want to see how you get on at that level. We can't move too fast. You'll have to be patient.'

Wayne knew he could be patient. He could be

anything if it meant playing for the Everton first team. He finished changing out of his kit and headed for the showers. The hot water felt good after playing on a rainy night.

As he put on his trousers and his Everton blazer, he was still floating on air. He felt a bit dizzy. His coach then gave a short speech which was greeted with some half-hearted clapping, but Wayne couldn't remember a single word of it. His mind was elsewhere, dreaming about what lay ahead. Maybe the nerves would come later but, for now, it was just pure excitement. He did, however, feel a bit guilty to be feeling so happy when the rest of his his teammates all looked so miserable.

But it was only natural that he felt excited. It meant that when the Premier League fixture list was released, Everton's games would be *his* games. If he proved himself, he might get to play at Old Trafford and Anfield. It was going to be easy to motivate himself over the summer. By the time that pre-season training was due to begin in July, he would be raring to go.

Over and over again, he kept replaying David

Moyes's words. *You'll be training with the first team next season. You'll be training with the first team next season.*

For a second, he thought about keeping it a secret and announcing it when the whole family would be together. After all, his aunts, uncles and cousins had all played their part in encouraging him over the years. But once he saw his dad waiting outside the Villa Park ground in the car park, he knew he couldn't delay telling someone. Confident that the team bus wouldn't leave without him, he raced over to share the news with him.

After seeing Aston Villa lift the Cup Final trophy, Big Wayne was expecting his son to be quiet or angry or both. Instead, he had a grin plastered all over his face.

'Wayne, have you forgotten the final score?'

'Of course not, but I just got some news that trumps that. David Moyes came to see us after the game. He took me aside and told me I would be promoted to the first team next season. I'm going to be training with my heroes! Can you believe that?!'

Big Wayne's eyes lit up. He was speechless for a moment. Then he just pulled his son towards him and gave him a big bear hug. 'A Rooney playing for Everton! You deserve it, son. Wow, this is a day you'll never forget. I certainly won't forget it.'

The horn on the bus sounded and Wayne saw that they were all waiting for him. The driver was waving for him to hurry up. They had a long drive ahead and it was already late.

'Dad, I've got to go but I'll see you at home. I'll tell you about the rest of the conversation then. Thanks for coming down for the game. Sorry we didn't put on a better show.'

As Wayne walked away towards the bus, he wondered if he'd spotted a tear in his father's eye. 'I'm proud of you, son!' Big Wayne called out. Then he climbed into his car, turned the music up loud and started his drive home, smiling all the way.

CHAPTER 13

IN DREAMLAND WITH COLLEEN

Over the years, Wayne got to know all of the neighbours in his street. Most of the boys had played football together outside, or at The Gems – before school, after school and into the evening until it got too dark.

But there was one particular neighbour that Wayne did not get to see as often as he wanted – Colleen McLoughlin. She was one of the prettiest girls he had ever seen, and the McLoughlin and Rooney families knew each other well. In fact, Wayne's cousin Claire was one of her friends. The two families met up a few times a year for barbeques and birthday parties. The McLoughlins were Liverpool fans, but any rivalry was friendly.

Even though the families were friends, though, Colleen didn't speak to Wayne much. He wasn't sure why. Maybe it was because he had accidently broken her brother's tennis racket a few years ago. He had apologised and explained how it happened but she obviously hadn't forgotten it.

Colleen was never rude to Wayne, though; she just had different interests and she chose to spend her time with other girls. When he was playing football, she was usually at a dance practice or an acting lesson.

Unfortunately for Wayne, his progress through the ranks at Everton would not be enough to win her heart. He knew her brothers but she didn't usually hang around with them. And the few times that she did come and watch the football in the street, she didn't seem impressed by Wayne's attempts to show off.

It was going to take something special to attract her attention.

'Oh come on, get me a date with her,' he begged her brothers on a regular basis. 'She doesn't care about me playing for Everton. I don't know how else to impress her.'

They passed on the message. 'Tell Wayne he can call me if he wants to ask me out,' Colleen told her brothers. 'He shouldn't get you to do it for him.'

'Why don't you come and see him tomorrow night? We'll be playing footie again after school.'

'I can't. I have a dance class. But I've seen him in the streets, yelling and showing off. All he talks about is football. I don't like boys like that.'

A few weeks later, though, the perfect moment finally came about. Wayne was busy doing what he usually did on a week night – playing football in the street. Then two girls appeared on a bike. And one of them was Colleen.

With sweat pouring down his face, scuffed shoes and a bloody cut on his elbow, Wayne realised he didn't look his best. Not that he ever spent much time styling his hair or picking out fancy clothes. That just wasn't him.

'Hi, Colleen,' he called, pushing other boys aside to make sure she saw him.

Colleen waved back, but she was distracted by a problem with the bike. Something was wrong – Wayne thought maybe a tyre was flat or the brakes had given up. He was worried for her. Colleen pushed the bike on to the pavement and approached Wayne, who was with one of her brothers.

'Can you take a look at the bike? The chain keeps catching and we're afraid it's going to snap off. Dad will be furious if I've broken it already.'

Wayne knew this was his chance. 'I'll fix it,' he said, before anyone could either offer to help or point out that he was a disaster when it came to fixing anything.

Colleen's admirer looked closely at the chain. It was just as he thought – he had no idea what was wrong or how to fix it. But Colleen needed his help. She was depending on him.

'Don't worry. I'll hook it back on. Just give me two minutes.'

Ten minutes later, after trying everything else he

could think of, Wayne finally struck gold. The chain clicked back into place and the bike was good as new.

Colleen ran over and hugged Wayne, who went bright red.

'Want to go for a walk?' he mumbled.

Colleen thought about it. She owed him that at least. 'Sure, but I've got to be home for dance class by eight.'

For Wayne, training with Everton was great but spending time with Colleen was just as good, maybe even better. In some ways, they didn't have much in common. But conversation came easily and naturally. He couldn't stop staring at her. They talked about all kinds of things, and he was determined to show her that he wasn't just the loud boy who played football in the street.

'That's not how I am all the time. I'll prove it to you. I'm a bit cocky when I'm playing football, that's all.'

Colleen smiled. She was starting to appreciate Wayne's gentler side.

'You're saying all this but how do I know if I can believe you?' she asked, winking at him.

'Easy. Let me take you to see a film at the weekend. I'll be on my best behaviour. You can even pick the film.'

'I see what you're trying to do.' She laughed. 'I guess I'll have to go on a proper date with you to find out then.'

It was all going to plan. He would do anything to spend more time with Colleen. With every minute he spent with her, Wayne liked her more and more.

But now it was time to walk Colleen home, and he needed to make her aware of how much he liked her. When they passed behind a building, out of sight of the neighbours, he leaned in and kissed her. Colleen kissed him back. Wayne was in dreamland.

When they said goodnight, Wayne promised to call the next day to arrange their date at the weekend.

'I'm looking forward to it,' she said. 'Just don't wear your Everton kit!' She went inside and then waved to Wayne from the window.

Wayne skipped all the way home. His prayers had been answered. He had a chance with Colleen.

CHAPTER 14

FIRST STEPS IN THE FIRST TEAM

Wayne had been waiting all summer for pre-season training to start, but finally he was on the way to Bellefield, then Everton's training ground. Big Wayne insisted on driving him there – and Wayne suspected that his dad probably hoped to stick around and watch the sessions.

He was surprised that he didn't feel more nervous. But he really felt sure that he was good enough to train with the first team. He had watched a lot of Everton games last season and thought he could make a difference. Naturally, his family agreed.

'I reckon it'll take about a week for Moyes to see that you need to be starting,' Uncle Eugene said.

'Duncan Ferguson and Kevin Campbell are nearing the end of their careers. Both of them have been great for Everton but it's time to look to the future.'

Wayne's first stop on arriving at Bellefield was the reception counter. He had papers to fill out and he had to pick up his training kit. But as he was not yet even seventeen, or eligible for a driving licence, he wouldn't need a parking space.

He found out that he had been given the number 18 shirt for the 2002/03 season. It had been Paul Gascoigne's number last season so Wayne was stepping into big shoes. He was too young to have seen all of Gazza's career but he knew what a great player he was.

Manager David Moyes brought Wayne into the dressing room and did some introductions, even though the youngster recognised everyone in the squad and they had clearly all heard about him.

The Everton players were very welcoming. Well, most of them were. A few teased him about his clothes, but if they had expected Wayne to come into the squad and be shy or quiet, they thought wrong.

He was one of the loudest in the dressing room from day one.

Once training started, Wayne proved that he belonged. He came alive when the coaches set up a 'forwards-against-defenders' session. He got a few strong 'welcome to the first team' tackles from David Unsworth and David Weir. But he responded by nutmegging Unsworth and firing a shot into the bottom corner. He then muscled Weir off the ball and hit the post with a volley.

'Nice shot,' Mark Pembridge shouted. 'You play like a pitbull so we'll call you Dog from now on. Everyone has to have a nickname.' The nickname stuck.

Wayne played with a swagger but he worked hard too. By the end of the first training session, other players had spotted his remarkable potential.

'Nothing scares you, does it?' Unsworth asked him. 'I thought you'd start moaning after you got a few bruises. I can't believe you're only sixteen.'

'It's a good test for me,' Wayne replied. 'Defenders

on other teams are going to kick me even harder. I'm not scared but I need to be ready.'

'Well, if you have any trouble, we'll have your back.'

The highlight of Wayne's first day was talking to Duncan Ferguson, his childhood idol. Ferguson walked over to say hello but, for the first time since he arrived, the younger player was nervous.

'I can't believe I'm training with you,' Wayne said with a shaky voice. 'You've been my hero for years. You probably wouldn't remember but I wrote you letters a few years ago and you took a photo with me and my brothers.'

'Thanks for making me feel old,' Ferguson said with a smile. 'I still like to think I'm one of the youngsters. I'm excited to see you play. Anything you need around here, just let me know. Do you play computer games?'

'Yeah, I love them. I'll play anything really.'

'Alright. First away game of the season, come to my room. But be warned – I'm the club champion. None of the other lads can beat me.'

A few weeks later at Bellefield, Wayne stunned everyone into silence when he chipped Richard Wright from an impossible angle. To him, it was just normal to attempt a shot from there. But Moyes and his coaches just looked at each other. They didn't need to say the words; their faces said it all.

'Do you think he meant that?' Wright asked at the end of the session. Unsworth was standing nearby. He nodded. 'Knowing Wayne, he meant it.'

Later that season, Moyes would tell Wayne: 'Looking back, that's when I knew you were going to make it in the first team.'

As Uncle Eugene had predicted, Wayne had made the Everton first team more unpredictable, and Moyes wanted to test his young star in the team's pre-season friendlies. Wayne was unstoppable, scoring nine goals. But the message remained: be patient.

The day after a friendly against Athletic Bilbao, Moyes called Wayne into his office.

'Great performance last night, Wayne. You'll get plenty of opportunities this season. But you won't be starting every game. Your career is only just beginning and I want to protect you and give you the chance to rest.'

'But I don't need time to rest. I just want to play.'

'I know – and we love that about you. But this is a big change for you. The Premier League is so physical. You're only sixteen years old and you're still developing.'

Wayne nodded, but he disagreed. Everton need me to start every game, he thought to himself. He decided it wasn't worth making a fuss about it yet. He just needed to play so well that Moyes couldn't even think about leaving him on the bench.

He kept working hard in training and it paid off. By the time the 2002/03 Premier League season kicked off, he had earned his place in the starting line-up. One day after training, Moyes called him into his office to share the news.

'You'll be starting up front with Kevin Campbell against Tottenham at the weekend. We think you're ready for this. I'm not telling the media yet so that they don't put too much pressure on you. But I wanted you to know. The biggest thing to remember is to just play your game. Don't let them get under your skin.'

Wayne's fierce competitiveness was often an issue. When things weren't going well, he sometimes lunged into a tackle. That had to stop. 'I won't let you down,' he promised. 'I can handle the pressure.'

He tried calling his parents with the big news of his first team debut, but couldn't reach them. When he got home, Graeme and John were just coming back from school.

'Oh wow, I think that's the Everton star Wayne Rooney!' John joked, shouting loudly down the street.

'It is! It is! It's really him! Can we have an autograph?' Graeme joined in. Both brothers couldn't stop giggling.

'Good one!' Wayne said, smiling. His brothers would never let him get too cocky. 'I've got a bit of news for you actually. I'm starting against Tottenham this weekend!'

Graeme and John rushed over to hug their brother.

'That's amazing news,' John said. 'Have you told Mum and Dad? We need to get tickets.'

'You're the first to know.'

They liked that. 'Can we sell the story to the newspapers?'

'Actually, you can't tell anyone. It's a secret at the moment.'

As the family sat down for dinner, Jeanette and Big Wayne were still shaking with excitement after hearing their son's news. Wayne watched how proudly his dad behaved, as he wandered around talking to other family members on the phone. There was no chance of this staying a secret for long.

Big Wayne lifted his beer glass. The rest of the family lifted their glasses too. 'Wayne, Saturday is going to be a very proud day for this family. Congratulations. You really deserve it, and there's no pressure, of course. We only expect you to score two goals!' They all laughed.

On the Saturday, Wayne's alarm sounded at 7 am. But it was hardly necessary. He had been awake for hours. Everyone had told him to savour every moment in the build-up to his first start for Everton, but now he was too pumped up to sleep. In the end, he gave up and went to watch television downstairs. Before long, the early morning football preview shows started, and he poured himself a glass of orange juice as he listened to a panel of former players making predictions for the day's games, including *his* game.

When the panel talked about Everton's match against Tottenham, Wayne was the first topic under discussion. The panel urged Everton fans not to expect too much, too soon from Wayne. After all, they said, he was a sixteen-year-old youngster who was totally unproven in the Premier League.

'Not for long,' Wayne muttered to himself. 'People are going to know my name soon.'

His thoughts were soon interrupted as the rest of the Rooneys joined him in front of the TV, all sharing in the excitement.

'Today's the day!' Big Wayne called out, rushing up to his son and patting his shoulder.

'Just remember, if you miss a sitter, everyone will see it on *Match of the Day*,' Graeme joked.

'And if I score a hat-trick, they'll see that as well!' Wayne shot back, though he was trying to hide the nerves that were building inside him. He didn't have an appetite for breakfast, even though his mum was offering to make anything he wanted.

On the way to the stadium, Wayne was unusually quiet. His dad glanced in the car's rear-view mirror a couple of times to check his son was okay.

Wayne was just doing a lot of thinking – mainly about all the moments that had led up to this moment. He was a sixteen-year-old about to make his Premier League debut for his boyhood club. It didn't get much better than that. He was living the dream of boys all over the country. He tilted his head back against the headrest and tried to put the emotions aside.

By the time they reached Goodison Park, he was ready. Nervous, excited, curious – but above all, ready for the challenge. His heart was beating fast at the buzz around the stadium, the music on the loudspeakers and the excited faces of the Everton fans.

And when he walked into the dressing room and saw the famous blue shirt hung up at his spot with Rooney on the back and the number 18 below it, he could not wait to put it on and make his debut.

The pitch looked in perfect condition, and the crowd was steadily growing. During the warm-up, he soaked up the atmosphere. He felt lots of eyes watching his every touch of the ball – or maybe it was just his imagination.

After Moyes's final words, Wayne and the rest of the Everton team walked out of the dressing room and into the tunnel. He looked at the experienced professionals all around him. In the Tottenham line stood Teddy Sheringham and Jamie Redknapp. A few of the players were old enough to be his father. He tried to look calm as he stood near the back of the Everton line. Kevin Campbell was just behind him, cracking jokes and helping to lighten the mood. 'Good luck today, Wayne. If you get a chance, don't hesitate to shoot,' he added. 'Just smash it in the top corner like you do every day in training.'

The atmosphere was unbelievable. Even before kick-off, it was so loud. Once the game was underway, the home fans cheered every time he got the ball. Wayne didn't let anyone push him around. A few of the Tottenham defenders tried to wind him up. They said it was a man's game and there was no place for a boy. Wayne took no notice. He had expected some nastiness. He had a target on his back as 'the next big thing' and defenders would want to make a statement.

It wasn't long before the fans were on their feet – and Wayne was part of the reason. His pass set up Pembridge to give Everton the lead. Pembridge ran straight to Wayne as he celebrated. 'Great assist, Dog,' he said, hugging Wayne.

With the score at 1-1 in the second half, Moyes took Wayne off. Wayne didn't complain but he was confused about the decision. 'I didn't understand that,' he told teammate Alan Stubbs after the game. 'I felt fresh. I wanted to score the winner.' He was sure he was playing well enough, and he wasn't tired. He was getting some rough tackles from the Tottenham defenders but he felt calm, and he wasn't going to lose his temper. But he tried not to let his frustration show when talking to Stubbs in case he seemed like a bad teammate.

It was a disappointing end to Wayne's debut but he would never forget the feeling of starting his first game for Everton. He just hoped that he would get more opportunities to show his talent.

CHAPTER 15

BECOMING AN INSTANT HERO

Wayne knew that he had a big moment just around the corner. That's what he kept telling anyone who doubted that he would make it. Like David Moyes kept saying, he just had to be patient. But it wasn't easy.

That big moment came a few weeks later when Arsenal came to town. It was another full house at Goodison Park and the Rooney family had landed a stack of tickets. But, for most of the day, Wayne could not hide his disappointment: he was going to be a substitute.

'I deserve to be starting,' he complained to his parents. 'Being young isn't a good reason to leave me out. If I'm good enough, I should be playing every game. I don't need rest. I could play a game every day and he thinks I can't play two games in a week.'

Usually, it was Big Wayne who stepped in for the pep talks that put his son back on track. But this time Jeanette had heard enough.

'Are you just going to sit here and sulk?' she scolded. 'You're a Rooney – that's not how we do it. We fight. Get out there and prove he made a mistake leaving you on the bench. Complaining won't get you anywhere. Let your feet do the talking.'

She's got a point, Wayne thought. If he gives me a chance today, that's exactly what I'll do.

Arsenal had put together a thirty-game unbeaten league run and they were the favourites to win the title. Everton had nothing to lose. Wayne tried to stay calm on the bench but, as the minutes ticked by, and the score reached 1-1, his frustration grew. He felt restless. As a distraction, he tried to look for his family in the crowd. He was sure that he could make a difference. Maybe he would come on for the last thirty minutes.

But the clock ticked on. Thirty minutes to go. Twenty minutes to go. Finally, with barely ten minutes to go, he was called to replace Tomasz Radzinski. After a quick warm-up, he was part of the game at last.

'Get stuck in and don't be afraid to take them on,' Alan Stubbs told him, putting an arm on his shoulder. 'They're tired. You'll be sharper than them.'

Wayne felt alive and he was at the centre of the action, winning tackles and making runs. The crowd was suddenly interested again and roared, as if he had woken them from a nap.

Then came the moment that catapulted him into the spotlight. Thomas Gravesen lobbed the ball towards him and it dropped to him twenty-five yards out. Wayne didn't hesitate. He did what he had always done – he let his instincts take over. He turned, dribbled and saw that no Arsenal players were closing him down. He didn't need a second invitation, and so fired a booming shot towards the Arsenal goal.

His heart skipped a beat the second it left his

foot. 'I couldn't have hit it any sweeter,' he told his parents later. The shot rocketed over the head of goalkeeper David Seaman, off the underside of the crossbar, and into the roof of the net.

Wayne didn't have time to think about his goal celebration. Pure joy took over. The crowd erupted. Fans were screaming, jumping, hugging. Everyone on the Everton bench was on their feet. So was Ray Hall, who had moved so quickly to sign Wayne for the Centre of Excellence, and who was also at Goodison Park that afternoon. Wayne's teammates raced after him and jumped on his back. It was a blur – just blue everywhere.

With just one kick of the ball, all Wayne's anger and frustration had been replaced with euphoria and triumph. Up in the crowd, Jeanette sobbed with pride. At the final whistle, the Everton fans chanted 'Roo-ney!' at the tops of their voices.

After the final whistle, it was all about Wayne. Moyes hugged him and his teammates gave him high fives until his palms stung. Every question, every conversation, every story was about Wayne.

Arsene Wenger was quick to praise the young match-winner. It meant a lot to Wayne that the Arsenal manager called him the best English player he had seen since taking the job at Highbury back in 1996.

And Wayne's goal had set yet another record. He was the youngest ever Premier League goalscorer. He hadn't even turned seventeen yet.

After the game, Wayne went to the pub with his dad. The locals couldn't believe it when the match-winner walked through the door. 'Wayne, you're a star now,' the owner said. 'You won't be able to have a quiet drink ever again.' Everyone wanted a word with him, asking him to describe the goal for them and telling him that he was going to lead Everton to lots of trophies. When it was time to leave, he had to push his way through the crowds to reach the door.

By the time *Match of the Day* began that night, celebrations at the Rooneys' house were in full swing. As Wayne's wonder strike was replayed from every angle, each family member wanted to have the last word.

'What a hit!'

'That's a definite goal of the season contender.'

'Yeah, and look at the crossbar shake after Wayne's shot.'

Wayne sat quietly, only half listening to the conversation. He was emotionally and physically drained. Sure, he'd only played for ten minutes in that Arsenal game, but it was the most dramatic ten minutes of his life. It definitely hadn't sunk in yet, but he got the sense that life would never be the same again. When he woke up the next morning, it all felt like a dream.

CHAPTER 16

CHEWING HIS WAY INTO TROUBLE

Drops of sweat formed on Wayne's forehead. It was so hot. Didn't they have air conditioning in here?

He had been thrilled when he heard that he was nominated in the Young Sports Personality category at the BBC Sports Personality of the Year awards. It meant a trip to London, staying in a fancy hotel and getting to meet some of the top athletes in the world.

He called Colleen straightaway.

'How do you fancy a night in London next month?'

'What? Are you serious?'

'You bet. What do you think? The *Sports*

Personality of the Year show is in a couple of weeks and I'm up for an award.'

'Congratulations, babe. That's amazing. I'd love to go. Let me speak to Mum and Dad about it. I'll need to buy a new dress, of course!'

A romantic trip and the possibility of winning another award. This was going to be great, Wayne thought.

But Everton had other ideas. They told Wayne after a training session that Colleen could not go with him to the event. Wayne was furious and stormed home. He went for a long walk to calm down but it didn't really help.

'It was none of their business!' he shouted when his mum asked about it. 'It's not an Everton event. I can't believe this.'

'What was the reason?'

'Apparently, it would send the wrong message. Colleen had bought a dress and shoes. Now she'll have to return them. She's going to be crushed.'

Wayne considered not attending the event as a protest. But in the end he travelled down to London and checked in at one of the most expensive hotels he had ever seen. He was afraid to touch anything. 'I'm just glad that I won't be paying the bill,' he told his mum.

When he arrived for the event, he saw famous athletes everywhere he looked. Lennox Lewis and Steve Redgrave were standing on one side of the room. Paula Radcliffe was there too. He just wasn't sure what to say to them. Would they even know who he was? He went to get a drink and then took his seat.

As he sat in the audience, Wayne was nervous about all the cameras that were pointing at him. He opened a pack of chewing gum to calm his nerves. At least he'd have fresh breath, if one of the presenters came over to interview him.

Finally, the winners were announced. The nominations for the Young Sports Personality of the Year award had been narrowed down to three – shooter Charlotte Kerwood, gymnast Becky Owen and Wayne. The fact that England's football manager Sven-Goran Eriksson was presenting the trophy was a big clue. He opened the envelope and called out Wayne's name.

Wayne gave a big smile for the cameras as he walked onto the stage. The trophy felt heavy. He delivered a short speech – he had prepared a lot more but with the cameras and lights and such a huge audience, he was shaking and just wanted to get off the stage without saying anything embarrassing.

As he returned to his seat, he realised he had forgotten about the gum he'd still been chewing. Maybe no one had noticed.

No such luck. As he got changed in his room afterwards, his phone rang.

'Wayne, what were you thinking chewing gum like that on national television?!' his mum asked.

'Mum, I forgot. Everything was a blur. Aren't you going to congratulate me on the award?'

Jeanette paused. 'Yes, of course, we're very proud of you. I'm just saying that chewing gum really didn't look good.'

Wayne hung up. He didn't want to talk about it.

The next day, to his disbelief, the gum-chewing became a national story.

He called Colleen. 'Have you seen the papers? Why is this such a big deal?'

'Ignore it, Wayne. They're just trying to sell papers. This is what happens when people decide you're a celebrity.'

'But they're making it sound like I don't know any better; like I have no manners. I heard someone saying I didn't do my tie up properly either. I'm still a kid – why do they expect me to be perfect?'

It just seemed so unfair. He wasn't used to speaking in front of big audiences or wearing a suit. It was normal to make mistakes.

'People can be cruel,' Colleen said. 'You won the trophy – focus on that.'

Wayne said nothing.

'You're going to need a bigger room to store all your trophies,' she joked, trying to change the subject.

It was all a learning experience for Wayne. He had been the golden boy for months but now he understood how quickly things could change.

CHAPTER 17

ENGLAND'S NEWEST SUPERSTAR

Wayne was proud to be English. He always had been. Playing for England, though? Well, he hadn't really thought that far ahead. He had dreamed of scoring crucial goals for England – like Michael Owen had done against Argentina and David Beckham against Greece – but he understood that he needed to make his mark at Everton first. As Moyes kept saying, he needed to be patient and remember that his whole career was ahead of him. There were no shortcuts.

Wayne was happy to take it step by step. If he could impress at Everton, he might get a call to join the Under-21s. And if he shone for the Under-21s, he might eventually get Sven-Goran Eriksson's

attention and join the senior team. Maybe that
would happen in time for the 2006 World Cup
in Germany.

One morning, Wayne was training with his
Everton teammates. He ran a couple of laps of the
pitch and went through a few stretches. While some
of his older colleagues seemed to need a long warm-
up to loosen up their bodies, he felt fresh from the
start. He could play a match every day of the week.

As he waited, Moyes wandered over to him and
handed him an orange bib ready for the first passing
drill. He grabbed Wayne's arm and guided him over
to the touchline.

'Is something wrong?' Wayne asked.

Moyes grinned. 'No, Wayne. Nothing to worry
about. Quite the opposite, actually. I just got a call.
You've been picked for England. Congratulations!'

A huge smile broke out across Wayne's face. He
was being noticed. This was the first step. He was
still just seventeen and now he was going to be in
the Under-21 squad.

'That's amazing. Who are we playing?'

Moyes looked puzzled, as if the question had caught him by surprise. 'I thought you'd know the answer to that. It's Australia at Upton Park.'

'What?! The senior team? I thought you meant the Under-21s!'

Wayne went silent for a second, still in shock. His legs turned to jelly. The senior squad? Really? He'd be sharing a dressing room with some of the biggest names in the Premier League?

He mumbled his way through the rest of the conversation, thanked Moyes and rejoined the training session with his head still spinning.

'What was that all about?' asked Mark Pembridge, who had been standing closest to Wayne and Moyes.

'I got called up by England for the Australia friendly,' Wayne replied. He couldn't say the words without smiling.

'Lads, Dog's in the England squad for Wednesday night.'

The other players gathered round and congratulated Wayne.

'Can you get your mum's permission to be out

that late on a school night?' Unsworth asked, jabbing Wayne playfully in the ribs.

'Yeah, maybe she can write you a note!'

'Wayne, just to make sure your ego doesn't get too big, go and set up the orange cones on the edge of the box,' assistant manager Alan Irvine said with a grin.

Wayne laughed it off. He was used to this kind of teasing by now. It kept his feet on the ground. He knew his teammates were happy for him. They even planned a special announcement at lunch in the cafeteria, where they presented him with a carton of milk.

'Well, you can't have champagne yet, Wayne!' Pembridge said with a big grin as he handed Wayne the milk.

After lunch, he called his parents.

'England's number 9! England's, England's number 9!' Big Wayne couldn't resist singing that chant when he heard the news. 'Not many youngsters are so good that they skip the Under-21s. Sven must have been impressed.'

'I didn't even know he was watching me, to be honest. I'd never seen him at Goodison.'

A week later, Wayne's Uncle Eugene drove him to the hotel in London where the rest of the England squad was staying. By then, he had overcome the shock. He still had butterflies in his stomach but he felt convinced that he belonged in the squad.

The journey by car with Uncle Eugene was tiring, but Wayne still managed to stay awake for the team lunch. It was hard not to be star struck when he walked into the restaurant and saw David Beckham, Steven Gerrard, Paul Scholes and all the other big names. These were the players that he had grown up watching. Luckily, he wasn't the only new boy and he already knew Franny Jeffers who had come through the Everton youth system.

'Welcome to the squad, Wayne. Call me Stevie.'

Wayne turned around to find Steven Gerrard standing next to him. They shook hands and swapped stories from growing up in Liverpool. It was a relief to break the ice. It was easy to forget that the other players were just normal lads like him who loved playing football.

After lunch, he was ready for a quick nap before the mid-afternoon team meeting. He wanted to be as fresh as possible for the training sessions. As soon as his head hit the luxury hotel pillows, he fell fast asleep.

The next thing he knew, there were people in his room – someone from the hotel reception and two members of the coaching staff. He glanced at the clock. He had overslept and was late for the meeting!

'What happened?' one of the coaches asked angrily. 'Get yourself downstairs. We're all waiting for you.'

Wayne felt terrible. He was embarrassed and now all eyes would be on him when he tried to sneak in quietly at the back of the room. It was the worst way to start his England career, but luckily, the other players didn't give him a hard time.

Sven-Goran Eriksson spoke to the squad and explained that everyone would get some time on the pitch in the game against Australia.

'No one is going to play the whole game,' he said.
'I want to take a look at the starting eleven in the
first half and we'll bring out a different group for the
second half. You'll all get a chance to play. Enjoy it!'

Things got better once training started. Wayne
was eager to impress, hoping to get as much playing
time as possible in the friendly. He stole the show
in the shooting drills. Everything he hit ended up in
the top corner. David Seaman was soon sick of the
sight of Wayne!

'I'm going to have to retire if you keep smashing
shots past me,' he said, fishing another ball out of the
net and having flashbacks to Wayne's wonder goal.

'How does it compare to the Everton training?'
Gerrard asked Wayne.

'Everything is a lot quicker,' he replied, after
pausing for a minute to find the right words. 'I like
how creative it is. I'll be suggesting a few things
when I get back there.'

'I'm sure the coaches will be pleased to be told
that they need to do things differently,' Gerrard
joked.

The game against Australia was at Upton Park in east London, home to West Ham United. As Wayne sat down on the bench and heard the national anthem, he felt proud. If all went to plan, he would be making his England debut tonight!

But nothing went to plan for the home side in the first half. Australia scored twice and it was left to Wayne and some of the other newcomers to rescue England after half-time. He was so pumped up, he felt like he could run all day. As he stood in the centre circle ready for the start of the second half, he took a second to savour the moment – his England debut. He hoped it was the start of a long international career.

Wayne made an instant impact. His energy lifted his teammates and he set up a goal for Jeffers. In the end, England lost 3-1, but at least they had pulled a goal back in the second half, and Wayne's performance had been eye-catching.

In the dressing room, Wayne showed yet again that he didn't lack confidence. He started joking with the players who had started the game. 'Are you sure that you're the first team? Maybe we should start the next game.'

Paul Scholes just stared at him.

'Wayne, come back when you've won a few Premier League titles,' Gary Neville told him. Wayne couldn't tell if he was smiling.

Since arriving in London at the team hotel, everything had gone so fast that he hadn't even realised that he was making history. At seventeen years and 111 days old, he was now the youngest-ever player for England. He loved setting new records.

Much to Wayne's surprise, Gerrard appeared holding the matchball, signed by all the players. 'Great game, Wayne. This is just the beginning for you. You're going to be a star for England for many years to come.'

Wayne certainly hoped so. He had loved every minute of his first England cap. And even after just a couple of days testing himself against the country's best footballers, he felt that he had become a better player.

CHAPTER 18

JOY AND PAIN AT EURO 2004

Wayne's Everton teammates talked about summer breaks spent on the beach relaxing ahead of next season. He liked the sound of it, but plans like those would have to wait during the summer of 2004. The Rooneys had previously huddled around the television to watch Euro '96 and Euro 2000, and now Wayne would be spending the summer in Portugal, leading the charge for England at Euro 2004.

The young player reflected on his extraordinary rise. In the space of a year, Wayne had gone from wondering if he would get a call up to the Under-21 team to being one of the first names on Sven-Goran Eriksson's team sheet. On the downside, he was playing well enough for Everton but still not as regularly as he wanted. He had scored eight goals in his first season and ten in his second, even though he was often coming on as a substitute. Overall, though, it had been a good year, especially as he and Colleen were now engaged.

As he packed his suitcase for Portugal, he wondered what it would be like to represent England at a major tournament. He still got goosebumps every time he put on the famous white shirt and playing at Euro 2004 would be the biggest moment of his career.

He knew tournaments could be long. England would have a few days between games and he would feel restless waiting in the hotels. So he packed lots of CDs and as many films as he could find in the house. Hopefully that would keep him busy. He crossed his fingers that there would be a hairdryer in the room in case he couldn't sleep.

'Missing anything, Wayne?' Jeanette asked as she passed her son's bedroom and saw his suitcase on the bed.

'Probably,' Wayne replied. 'You know I'm not good at organising my things.'

'Have you got enough underwear?'

'Mum, get out!' Wayne shouted, going red.

By the time he and his England teammates arrived in Portugal, they were desperate to get started. He lay down on his bed and started thinking about their first game against France. The French team had a lot of stars. He loved watching Zinedine Zidane and Thierry Henry. But they would be the enemy on Sunday.

There was a knock at the door. It was Steven Gerrard and Michael Owen.

'Want to grab a massage, Wayne? We're heading down there now,' Gerrard said.

Wayne considered it. It was better than just sitting in his room. 'Sure. Sounds like a good distraction.'

'Bored already?'

He shrugged. 'Yeah, kind of. What do you do with all the time between games?'

'You'll get used to it. The massages are good. We play cards a lot too – you can join us tonight if you want. We normally meet in Michael's room after dinner.'

'And sleeping is always pretty good,' Owen added. 'It's so hot during training – like it was in South Korea and Japan. I've always had afternoon naps at the big tournaments.'

Before going to bed that night, Wayne called his parents. He had promised to give them regular updates after his arrival, and he assumed that he wouldn't be paying the phone bill.

'So, what's it like being an England star at a big tournament?' Big Wayne teased. 'What's the hotel like? Are they treating you like royalty?'

It was good to hear his dad's voice. 'I'm bored,' he admitted. 'I can't wait for the games to start. But the other lads have been great. The team spirit is really good. We know we're not the favourites but we feel confident we can surprise people.'

'And you're the secret weapon, son,' Big Wayne added. 'These teams will know all about Beckham, Owen and Gerrard, but they haven't played against you.'

Finally, Wayne got his wish. He was told to be in the hotel lobby by 3 pm ready for the coach that would take the players to the Estádio da Luz, home of Benfica. During the warm-up and in the dressing room, he was louder company than ever, and was probably annoying the other players. He was so fired up that he had to calm himself down. As he picked up a bottle of water in the dressing room, Beckham put an arm on his shoulder.

'Keep a calm head out there. They know you're a threat so they'll try and wind you up. That was me in 1998 against Argentina. Don't fall for it. Don't even get involved in it. Just play your game.'

Wayne nodded. Ever since his first game for the Everton youth team, his temper had been an issue. He always wanted to win – and sometimes he wanted to win too badly. He would get frustrated and would go in for a wild lunge or shove a defender to the ground. Now, just minutes before his European Championships debut, he reminded himself that he couldn't lash out and he couldn't let his teammates down. The stakes were too high.

Wayne put on his headphones and listened to some of his favourite songs. He was starting to understand that the waiting was one of the hardest parts of playing in big games.

Sven-Goran Eriksson walked into the room and closed the door. He kept the message simple. 'If we control Zidane, we win the game. When we win possession, move it fast. Look for Wayne as the outlet. These defenders will be scared of him. Let's go!'

The players cheered, some exchanged high fives, others jumped to their feet and started pacing – they were ready.

As Wayne took his place in the tunnel, he didn't even look at the French players lined up next to him. He just shut out all distractions and pictured himself scoring the winning goal. He could hear the noise in the stadium – the players weren't even on the pitch yet, but the atmosphere felt electric.

It only took about five minutes for Wayne to realise that his manager was right. The French defenders *were* scared of him. He could see it in their eyes. He felt quicker and stronger. They were making desperate tackles to stop him and yelling at each other. He was even more fired up when Frank Lampard's header gave England the lead. In the second half, the French defenders looked exhausted but Wayne had plenty of energy left.

When he spotted a long ball over the top of the defence, he turned and raced after it. He was ahead of Mikael Silvestre as he burst into the box. This was it – this was the goal he had pictured in his head so many times. But then Silvestre lunged in and tripped Wayne to the ground. It was a penalty.

Wayne leapt to his feet and pounded his chest. He was happy to have won a penalty but angry that he didn't have a chance to shoot. The England fans roared. Among some of the world's biggest stars, an eighteen-year-old was dominating the game.

Owen came rushing over to congratulate him and others followed. 'Great stuff, Wayne. They can't handle you.'

But Beckham's penalty was saved by Fabien Barthez. Wayne couldn't believe it. If he hadn't been fouled, he was sure he would have taken his chance. With just under fifteen minutes to go, the ball went out of play. Wayne turned and hung his head. Now he was being substituted. He didn't feel tired but he had to come off.

As he bit his fingernails on the bench, he watched a nightmare taking place on the pitch. First, Zidane curled in a last minute free-kick to make it 1-1. Then in the final seconds Gerrard misjudged a back pass, Henry was fouled by David James and Zidane scored the penalty. Game over.

Wayne couldn't believe it. His body went numb. He thought he could have scored on the counter-attack. Now he would never know if he could have made the difference.

The England dressing room was as quiet as a library. Wayne just stared at the ground. It was the cruellest way to lose. Gerrard was especially quiet, sitting with his head in his hands. 'Chin up, Stevie,' Wayne said. 'We'll get it back against Switzerland.'

Sven let the players recover from the shock. Then he rallied them. 'The result hurts but the performance was excellent. We've got two more games and we control our destiny.'

If England won their next two games, they would qualify for the quarter-finals. France had been their toughest opponent and England had almost won – that was a positive sign.

When Wayne woke up the next morning, the loss of the game against France still stung. But when he got out on the pitch for a light training session, he was ready to move on.

Four days later, he played one of the best games of his career. With new-found confidence in the France game, he played with no fear in the second game against Switzerland. It took twenty-three minutes for him to write his name into the history books yet again – this time as the youngest scorer in European Championship history. Owen crossed the ball and Wayne powered a header into the net. It all seemed to happen in slow motion for him – the ball floating towards him, leaping to head it, and then the net rippling.

He checked that he wasn't offside and then raced over to the England fans, showing off with a cartwheel. Beckham was the first to jump on his back, and then Gerrard screamed, 'Get in, Wazza' in his ear. Wayne wished he could see his family and his mates back home, all jumping up and down in celebration. There would be quite some party in Croxteth tonight.

In the second half, Wayne was the star man again, thumping a low shot that cannoned off the post then the goalkeeper and into the net. There was no fancy celebration this time – he just jogged over to the England bench with a big grin, as if to say 'These major tournaments are pretty easy'.

Back at the hotel, his phone buzzed. It was his parents.

'Incredible game, son. How does it feel to be the most popular Englishman in the world?'

Wayne laughed. 'This was the best day of my life. We're back on track and nothing can stop us now.'

'Wayne, you should have seen it. The whole street was out celebrating tonight. Flags and banners and hats. We were being congratulated by people we didn't even know!'

The delighted player remembered the crazy excitement during the last World Cup. Back then, he was one of the lads out in the street dancing around. What a difference two years made!

'Hang on, Wayne,' Jeanette said. 'Colleen's here.'

Wayne heard muffled noises as his mother passed the phone to Colleen. 'Wayne, you're a national hero,' she said, laughing. 'You were amazing. I should be used to it by now but it's still so strange to be watching you on television. Anyway, I'm sure you've got some celebrating to do. I just wanted to hear your voice. I miss you!'

'I miss you too. I'll call again tomorrow, I promise.'

As the tournament continued, Wayne had more surprises up his sleeve. If football fans weren't paying attention yet, they soon were after he scored two more goals against Croatia. England were in the quarter-finals.

'You were unstoppable, Wayne. Terrific game.' Sven said, patting him on the back. The England manager had hoped Wayne would play well but never imagined he would be this good. He had been one of the best players at the tournament so far.

Back in the dressing room, Wayne turned the music up loud and started dancing. 'Quarter-finals, baby!' he yelled. At first, his teammates just laughed at him but soon they were joining in.

Sven was already thinking about the next game. 'If Wayne keeps this up, we can go all the way,' he said to one of his coaches.

Wayne had never felt more confident on a football pitch. And he was doing it against some of the best players in the world. Maybe he was just fearless. Maybe his legs were just fresher. Maybe he should be thanking Moyes for limiting his playing time.

The quarter-finals saw England face Portugal. The hosts. Wayne didn't care. He loved it when the crowd was against him and he could silence them with a goal or two.

Portugal had done their homework. They knew Wayne was the danger man. But all the attention on him meant Owen could shine. And Owen put England ahead early in the game.

Then disaster struck for Wayne and his Euro 2004 dreams crumbled. He challenged for a loose ball and a defender collided with his foot. At first, he thought he was fine. But then the pain kicked in. It was too strong. He was in agony. As soon as he dropped to the turf, he knew his tournament was over.

As he limped to the bench, tears filled his eyes. How could this be happening? Back home, the Rooneys sat in silence, heads in their hands. In an instant, Wayne's luck had turned against him.

Even sitting on the bench to watch the rest of the game became too much for him. As the pain got worse, he was rushed to hospital for an X-ray and then went back to the hotel to see the end of the match. To make matters worse, England lost on penalties. Just like that, his dream of carrying England to the final was all over.

For the second time in the tournament, Wayne was left to wonder what would have happened if he had been on the pitch. He couldn't stop thinking about it. He checked his phone and saw lots of messages wishing him a speedy recovery, including one from Colleen: 'Thinking about you. We'll get through this together. Can't wait to see you.'

As his teammates faced the fact that they were heading home, Wayne lay in his hotel room and stared at the ceiling. He couldn't face packing his suitcase. That could wait until tomorrow.

CHAPTER 19

TIME FOR A FRESH START

Always a blue? Wayne kept asking himself that question. He had believed it for years, thinking he would be an Everton player for life. He had written it on a T-shirt and he had grabbed the badge on his team shirt after scoring a goal.

But now he wasn't so sure. Even after returning from his heroics at Euro 2004 and being named in the Team of the Tournament, he was miserable. And he couldn't hide it.

'What's wrong, Wayne?' Jeanette asked her son, when she saw him lying on the sofa watching television for the third afternoon in a row.

'Nothing.'

Jeanette shook her head. 'No, Wayne. I know something's bothering you. You've been miserable all week. It's not like you. You're usually buzzing at the start of a new season. Is it just the injury that's getting you down?'

'I want to leave Everton.' He just blurted it out. He hadn't planned to; it just slipped out.

Jeanette stopped folding towels and looked at Wayne in disbelief.

'You don't mean that. Don't let your dad hear you say that.'

'I'm serious. I need a change.'

'Have you told Colleen? What does she think?'

'I haven't told her yet. We can work that part out.'

'It'll be a big change.'

'Maybe it won't be that far. There are big teams near here.'

'Please tell me you aren't thinking of Liverpool.'

'No way,' Wayne replied. 'That's the one club I could never sign for.'

Telling his dad was a scarier job. Big Wayne didn't say anything at first. He was in shock. 'Everton put you on the map,' he stumbled. 'They believed in you from day one. This is your home. The fans love you but they'll never let you forget it if you walk away now.'

'I can't face another season, Dad. I need a change. Newcastle are interested, maybe others too.'

'Now you believe everything you read in the papers?'

'No, but after my goals at Euro 2004, teams will be interested in signing me.'

Eventually, Big Wayne shrugged and let out a loud sigh. 'I can see I'm wasting my breath. Just do this for me – give yourself a few days to think it over. If you still want to leave by the end of the week then we'll speak to your agent and see what the options are.'

Wayne knew that his father had dreamed of watching him play for Everton for the next ten years or more. He could see the pain on Big Wayne's face and knew this was breaking his heart. 'Thanks for supporting me, Dad. I know it was the last thing you wanted to hear.'

Later that week, Wayne met with Everton manager David Moyes. It was a difficult, uncomfortable conversation. Wayne explained to Moyes that he wanted to leave and that he needed a new challenge. He wasn't going to change his mind.

As Wayne recapped the conversation for his parents that night, Big Wayne forced a sad smile. It was tough to take, but he would support his son no matter what, even if his time as a blue was running out. 'Let's call your agent.'

Things got harder and harder for Wayne. The Everton fans took the news of his departure badly. As Wayne watched the games while he recovered from his injury, he heard the fans chanting that he was greedy. He had become the villain.

Newcastle were still interested and Wayne started to imagine playing at St James's Park in the black-and-white shirts. It was a big stadium, with over 50,000 seats, and he had heard lots of good things about how passionate the fans were.

But thirty miles away from Everton at Old Trafford in Manchester, important conversations were taking place. Sir Alex Ferguson was pleading his case to his bosses:

'This is the future of the club. Wayne could be a Manchester United player for fifteen years. You all saw him at Euro 2004. He's a man-child and he's going to be the best player in the Premier League in the next few years. Put him in our team with Scholesy, Giggsy and Ruud and we'll be unstoppable. If we want the trophy back, we need to open the chequebook.'

'What if we wait until January?' one of Ferguson's bosses replied. 'We can speak to Everton again then and see whether we can negotiate a cheaper price.'

'We can't afford to wait that long. Wayne won't be available in January. He's too good. We have to act now or we'll regret it for years. Newcastle are already making a bid.'

The debate took six hours spread over two days. But eventually Ferguson got the answer he wanted. He had the green light to make a bid for Wayne.

As the end of the transfer window edged closer, Wayne was getting fed up with all the uncertainty. He just wanted to be playing football. His foot was feeling a lot better but not strong enough to think about playing matches yet. He wasn't even sure if Everton wanted him to play. The worst part was that it was now the final week of August, and if no one bought him by the end of the month, he would be stuck at Everton until January.

Finally, his phone buzzed. It was his agent, Paul Stretford.

'Wayne, are you sitting down?'

'Yeah, I'm just watching a film.'

'Well, pause it.' Paul sounded stressed.

Wayne reached for the remote control. 'What's going on? What are Everton saying now?'

'They got a call last night about completing a deal.'

'Have Newcastle officially made the offer?'

'Yes, they confirmed that.'

'Okay, great.' Wayne got up and walked into the kitchen to get a glass of water. 'It's a good club. Let's do it.'

'Hold on. I'm not done yet. That wasn't the latest news,' his agent said, excitement in his voice. 'Manchester United have just made an offer as well.'

That got Wayne's attention. 'United? Seriously?' He had a hundred questions. This was the call he had been dreaming about. 'Oh wow, we've got to make that happen. Champions League football and a chance to win trophies every season – that's where I want to go.'

'I thought you'd say that. How soon can you get to Manchester?'

Wayne laughed. Five minutes ago he was sulking and now he was talking about signing at Old Trafford. 'I'd walk all the way there if I had to. When would I sign the contract?'

'If the deal is done tonight, United want you there tomorrow afternoon.'

'No problem,' Wayne replied. He hung up and started making calls – his parents, Colleen, his cousins, his aunts and uncles. It had to be kept a secret, but Wayne was hours away from joining one of the biggest clubs in the world.

CHAPTER 20

A DREAM DEBUT

Recovering from his broken foot had been exhausting and lonely for Wayne. All he could do was spend early mornings in the gym, eat healthily to stay fit and watch games from the crowd as the new season began.

But it gave him plenty of time to dream about his United debut. He wanted to prove that Sir Alex Ferguson was right to spend big money to bring him to Old Trafford.

Some had said it would take time for him to return to his Euro 2004 form, but Wayne was fired up. 'They don't know me. If they did, they'd know I'm going to be even better.'

On 28 September 2004, he played his first game for Manchester United against the Turkish team Fenerbahce. What did he have up his sleeve? How about a hat-trick? It took only seventeen minutes for him to score his first United goal. There was a real release of emotion – a combination of the joy of scoring on his debut and the relief of being back to doing what he loved most. The injury had been heartbreaking but he was making up for lost time. The big price tag might have been stressful for some players but Wayne hadn't ever really worried about that. He just knew he would score bags of goals for United.

He wasn't satisfied with just one goal on his debut, though. Later in that first half, Ryan Giggs fed the ball to him outside the box and Wayne drilled a low shot into the bottom corner.

His confidence was sky high. When United won a free-kick thirty yards out, Giggs prepared to take it. But Wayne had other ideas. 'Let me have it. I want my hat-trick.'

Giggs smiled. He admired the youngster's

confidence. Ever since he'd walked into the United dressing room, he'd acted like he belonged.

Wayne lined it up, looked at the wall and curled a perfect free-kick past the Fenerbahce goalkeeper. Old Trafford erupted. He couldn't stop grinning. His performance had outdone even his wildest dreams.

After the game, all the talk was about Wayne's hat-trick. Was it the best United debut ever? Was he the best player in the Premier League? He celebrated the moment but reminded himself it was just one game.

Sir Alex Ferguson came over and shook Wayne's hand. 'That was some way to introduce yourself to the United fans! Terrific performance. We're going for all the trophies this season and you'll be a big part of that.'

'Bring it on!' Wayne said. 'I just want to win. I want to become a better player as well, but most of all I want to be a champion.'

'Well, you picked the right club then.'

Wayne smiled. It had been quite a night and he was looking forward to meeting up with his family.

But most of all, he couldn't wait for everything that lay ahead for him in a United shirt.

'Welcome aboard, Wayne,' Ferguson said with a big smile as he walked out of the dressing room. 'It's going to be a heck of a ride.'

WAYNE ROONEY'S HONOURS

Manchester United

★ Premier League: 2006–07, 2007–08, 2008–09, 2010–11, 2012–13

★ League Cup: 2005–06, 2009–10

★ FA Community Shield: 2007, 2010, 2011

★ UEFA Champions League: 2007–08

★ FIFA Club World Cup: 2008

Individual

★ PFA Players' Player of the Year: 2009–10

★ PFA Young Player of the Year: 2004–05, 2005–06

★ PFA Fans' Player of the Year: 2005–06, 2009–10

★ PFA Premier League Team of the Year: 2005–06, 2009–10, 2011–12

★ Football Writers' Player of the Year: 2009–10

★ Sir Matt Busby Player of the Year: 2005–06, 2009–10

★ BBC Young Sports Personality of the Year: 2002

★ FIFPro World Young Player of the Year: 2004–05

★ Barclays Premier League Player of the Year: 2009–10

★ England Player of the Year: 2008, 2009, 2014
FIFA/FIFPro World XI: 2011

BIBLIOGRAPHY

Ferguson, Sir Alex, *My Autobiography* (London, Hodder Paperbacks, 2014)

Rooney, Wayne, *My Story So Far* (London, HarperSport, 2006)

Rooney, Wayne, *My Decade in the Premier League* (London, HarperSport, 2012)

Articles

Rooney, Copplehouse

Drayton, John, 'United and England star Rooney rolls back the years with youth team picture' (*Daily Mail*, Web: 27 March 2014):

http://www.dailymail.co.uk/sport/football/article-2590826/Manchester-United-England-star-Wayne-Rooney-rolls-years-youth-team-picture.html

Rooney, scouted by Everton
'Wayne Rooney: The making of a legend' (*The
Independent*, Web: 24 October 2006):
http://www.independent.co.uk/sport/football/
premier-league/wayne-rooney-the-making-of-a-
legend-421404.html

Ray Hall on Rooney
'How I found Wayne Rooney' (YouTube, Web:
uploaded 2 August 2010):
https://www.youtube.com/watch?v=CXUG5qc4sqo

Rooney's four goals at Euro 2004
'Euro 2012: Wayne Rooney's four goals at Euro
2004' (BBC Sport, Web: 19 June 2012):
http://www.bbc.com/sport/0/football/18502348

Young Sports Personality of the Year
'Rooney voted top youngster' (BBC Sport, Web: 8
December 2002):
http://news.bbc.co.uk/sport2/hi/special_events/
sports_personality_2002/2556671.stm

Rooney and superstitions
Winter, Henry, 'Wayne Rooney and Paul Gascoigne
may be rough diamonds but England need more
gems like them' (*Daily Telegraph*, Web: 10 January
2012):
http://www.telegraph.co.uk/sport/football/players/
wayne-rooney/9004066/Wayne-Rooney-and-Paul-
Gascoigne-may-be-rough-diamonds-but-England-need-
more-gems-like-them.html

David Moyes on Rooney
Burt, Jason, 'David Moyes Exclusive: The day I
realized Wayne Rooney would become a superstar'
(*Daily Telegraph*, Web: 11 October 2014): http://
www.telegraph.co.uk/sport/football/teams/
manchester-united/11155809/David-Moyes-
exclusive-The-day-I-realised-Wayne-Rooney-would-
become-a-superstar.html

Rooney returns to old primary school
Hughes, Lorna, 'Wayne Rooney returns to his old primary school ahead of winning his 100th England cap' (*Liverpool Echo*, Web: 11 November 2014): http://www.liverpoolecho.co.uk/news/liverpool-news/wayne-rooney-returns-old-primary-8093632

Rooney, goal vs. Arsenal
Haylett, Trevor, 'Wayne Rooney scores stunning goal for Everton against Arsenal to announce himself to the game: original report' (*Daily Telegraph*, Web: October 2002; republished 19 October 2012): http://www.telegraph.co.uk/sport/football/teams/everton/9612595/Wayne-Rooney-scores-stunning-goal-for-Everton-against-Arsenal-to-announce-himself-to-the-game-original-report.html

The real Wayne Rooney
McGarry, Ian, 'The real Wayne Rooney' (BBC Sport, Web: 7 November 2010): http://news.bbc.co.uk/sport2/hi/football/teams/m/man_utd/9164536.stm

Rooney signs for Manchester United
'Man Utd sign Rooney' (BBC, Web: 31 August 2004):
http://news.bbc.co.uk/sport2/hi/football/eng_prem/3611234.stm